Tim Harford's column, 'The Undercover Economist', which reveals the economic ideas behind everyday experiences, is published in the *Financial Times*. He is also the only economist in the world to run a problem page, 'Dear Economist'. Tim presented the BBC television series *Trust Me, I'm an Economist* and now presents the BBC radio series *More or Less*. His writing has appeared in *Esquire*, *Forbes*, *New York* magazine, the *Washington Post*, and the *New York Times*. Tim won the 2006 Bastiat Prize for economic journalism and is also an award-winning speaker.

D1346995

Also by Tim Harford

The Undercover Economist
The Logic of Life

DEAR UNDERCOVER ECONOMIST

ECONOMIST

**The very best letters from the
'Dear Economist' column**

TIM HARFORD

ABACUS

First published in Great Britain in 2009 by Little, Brown
This paperback edition published in 2010 by Abacus
Reprinted 2011

A CIP catalogue record for this book
is available from the British Library.

ISBN 978-0-349-12154-3

Typeset in Janson Text by M Rules
Printed and bound in Great Britain by
Clays Ltd, St Ives plc

Papers used by Abacus are from well-managed forests
and other responsible sources.

MIX
Paper from
responsible sources
FSC
www.fsc.org   FSC® C104740

Abacus
An imprint of
Little, Brown Book Group
100 Victoria Embankment
London EC4Y 0DY

An Hachette UK Company
www.hachette.co.uk

www.littlebrown.co.uk

To Fran

CONTENTS

Introduction

Can Economics Make You Happier?

Economists might not be the first people you would think of to give you advice on parenting, the intricacies of etiquette or the dark arts of seduction. Even at best the economist can seem a remote figure: infinitely rational, untroubled by indecision or weakness of the will, a Spock-like creature too perfect to be able to relate to mere human concerns. At worst the economist can look like a social naïf, if not an outright sociopath; a man (or occasionally a woman) who knows the price of everything and the value of nothing.

At least such is the traditional image of the economist; and who is Dear Economist to disappoint? He is not, it would be fair to say, as sympathetic as more traditional agony aunts. He is blunt. He is rude. He loves jargon. When confronted with a woman who enjoys the dating game but worries that she might leave it too late to settle down, Dear Economist offers not a shoulder to cry on but a frank explanation of optimal experimentation theory. When a dinner party guest wonders how much to spend on a bottle of wine, Dear Economist ignores the *Good Wine Guide* and reaches for the *Journal of Wine Economics*.

And yet his advice can be surprisingly sound. In the six years since the *Financial Times* entrusted me with the awesome responsibility of answering letters to Dear Economist, I have even – whisper it – been known to take some of his counsel myself.

1

This shouldn't be surprising. While Dear Economist's bedside manner may leave something to be desired, economics itself is remarkably well suited to the agony genre. The economist's instinct to strip away social niceties and model problems simply can succeed in providing just the kind of no-nonsense counsel we expect from any good advice column. And modern economics is far removed from its traditional image. It is no longer dominated by unworldly mathematical supermen but by streetwise statistical detectives, and the debate between behavioural economists and rational choice theorists is throwing ever more light on what rational economic behaviour looks like when people behave less like Mr Spock and more like Homer Simpson.

As a result modern economists understand much about both how we should behave and how we sometimes fall short. If anyone is going to dispense advice with the supreme confidence of the super-rational know-it-all, who better than an economist?

Should I Fake My Orgasms?
Love and Dating

It is not for nothing that sex, dating and relationships have traditionally formed the staple of the agony column. Wise words on these subjects are not easy to find. Not many people want to ask their parents for tips about losing their virginity. It is no less embarrassing to seek the opinions of colleagues as one contemplates an extramarital affair. We know that envious friends may not always give us impartial advice when we wonder whether we have, at last, found 'the one'. What could be more welcome in such cases, then, than the cool counsel of economic rationality?

Economists, it is true, do not generally enjoy a reputation as lotharios – unsurprisingly, when the economist's response to the delicate question of faking orgasms is to reach for the analytical framework of a two-player signalling game. But economists do not dismiss love. On the contrary, we are unorthodox experts in the romantic arts. Economists understand decision-making in the face of uncertainty. We understand the dangerous blandishments of cheap talk and the value of binding commitments.

Above all, economists understand the concept of non-zero-sum games, interactions in which both sides can expect to benefit from the bargain. When it comes to love, you could even say that we economists are optimists.

My boyfriend and I have been seeing each other for a while, and last month he moved in with me. It seems sensible for us to put his flat on the market, but he's suggesting that we wait a while in case things don't work out. What would you advise?

– V.H., Leeds

Dear V.H.,

Modern living has made it so much more difficult to judge where you stand.

Mothers used to teach their daughters not to believe suitors' promises that they would still love them in the morning. Then, commitment was made in the form of a marriage proposal. But then courts in the US stopped allowing women to sue for 'breach of promise' – the polite way of describing the actions of a cad who proposes marriage, beds his fiancée, and then changes his mind. At that point it became traditional to back up those promises with diamonds, a girl's best friend.

Times have moved on and it is much more difficult for both men and women to gauge their partners' seriousness. But if you apply a spot of screening theory to your domestic situation you will discover exactly where you are. (Screening, the theory of which won *enfant terrible* Joe Stiglitz a share of the Nobel Prize in 2001, is the art of finding out hidden information by forcing people to act, rather than simply murmur sweet nothings.)

If your boyfriend is enjoying the perks of living with you but

5

lacks real commitment to your relationship, then he enjoys a high option value from owning a flat to which he can return. This is true even if he loves you but doubts the constancy of that love.

If, on the other hand, he is convinced that you will grow old together, the option value of a spare bachelor pad is minimal. The only reason for him to hold on to the flat is because he thinks it's a good financial investment. Pundits can argue about the merits of this, but clearly the potential rewards are trivial compared with the loss of his soulmate.

To screen for your boyfriend's type, you must demand that he sells his flat at once – claim that the *Financial Times* has been predicting a fall in prices, if you wish.

The art of successful screening is to impose a demand that one type of person is unwilling to meet. You don't want to be sharing a house with that type of person, so put your foot down.

Yours credibly, The Undercover Economist

Dear Undercover Economist,

I have a Valentine's Day problem.

I will be taking my sweetheart out for a romantic dinner and I know how it will conclude: Juliet will refuse dessert, I'll order a chocolate cake and she will proceed to eat most of it. I find it an infuriating habit. Can you offer me any advice?

– Romeo, Verona

Dear Romeo,

It is safe to say that you will never persuade Juliet to order her own dessert, and ordering two for yourself as a joke is likely to be lost on her. You must take the quantity of cake as fixed and your problem as simply one of division.

This problem is not insoluble if basic utility theory is inventively deployed. Normally utility theory allows us to choose between spending income on different goods. Your problem is how to choose between two goods: cake for you and cake for Juliet (which will also make you happy, since you love her). Your calculations are complicated by the fact that while Juliet enjoys eating cake, she also enjoys watching you eat cake. Each of you would, given the choice, eat only part of the cake and donate the other part to your lover. But how much to donate?

Fortunately the economist Ted Bergstrom tackled the necessary equations fifteen years ago. All you need to do is work out how strong your love is for Juliet, compared with your love for cake – and perform the same calculation for her. Substituting the result into Bergstrom's equations gives you the answer. If you both tend to prefer cake, you will have to split the difference and each concede some cake to the other. If you care little for cake but love to watch each other enjoying it, you will try to foist the cake on each other.

True selflessness comes when both agree, without haggling, what the ideal division of cake should be. Then love is in the air.

Yours altruistically, The Undercover Economist

Dear Undercover Economist,

I am seventy-four, vigorous, wealthy and boringly married. My girlfriend of eight years, who is thirty-seven, has found a man of her own age of moderate means. She has assets of £300,000 and a salary of about £50,000. I had intended to give her £250,000 and would still do so if she continued a discreet relationship with me. What do you think?

— Mr Smith, London

Dear Mr Smith,

Your plan must overcome two obstacles. First Milton Friedman's 'permanent income hypothesis' invites us to consider any temporary windfall in terms of the income it could generate in perpetuity. In 2004 your payment of £250,000, while substantial, would have generated a permanent income of roughly £5,000 at prevailing real interest rates. This is only a modest sum compared with your girlfriend's salary, although perhaps less modest if she proposes starting a family and living off the income of her new beau for several years. In other words your offer is serious money to her only if she plans to make a serious commitment to her other relationship – an unfortunate combination for you.

There is a second concern – you cannot write an enforceable contract setting out what you expect for your considerable outlay. It is true that many romantic and sexual relationships have a financial component. However, not many succeed on the terms you propose – they either proceed to implicit long-term contracts, or else are carried out as, ahem, spot market transactions.

You may find it distasteful to pay your girlfriend by the hour or day. Even if you do not, she will. You are likely to have more success sticking to the formula that has stood you in good stead for eight years: keep hold of your money but turn on the charm.

Yours discreetly, The Undercover Economist

Dear Undercover Economist,

I've kissed a few boys in my time and I plan to kiss a few more. Eventually, however, I'd like to settle down and have children. How long should I leave it?

– Caroline Breyer, Manchester

Dear Miss Breyer,

Your candid query requires a non-trivial application of optimal experimentation theory. Start with a simpler variant: when visiting a regular restaurant haunt, at what point should you stop trying new dishes and simply order your favourite every time?

The answer depends on how much you like your favourite dish, your taste for variety and how many times you plan to return. If you plan to return often, it's worth encountering many disappointments on your quest to find a dish which surpasses your previous favourite. If the restaurant is soon to close down, it's better to stick to your preferred dish for the few visits you have left.

9

A similar calculation applies to your question, which is complicated by the fact that you do not know with certainty either your rate of accrual of men, nor the date at which you can no longer have children. But assume that you are able to 'sample' one man every two months and decide that whatever happens, you will settle down by thirty-five. At the age of eighteen, you have 102 men to look forward to and should only settle down if you happen upon one in the top 1 per cent.

If the years roll by without the appearance of Brad Pitt, you lower your critical threshold. You'll be encouraged to know that you can keep experimenting throughout your twenties without greatly lowering your standards. Even at thirty, a top 3 per cent man will do. But do not wait for ever. You may have to settle for an economist.

Yours experimentally, The Undercover Economist

Dear Undercover Economist,

I love my partner, but he does not always satisfy me in bed. Sometimes I fake my orgasms – is this wrong?

– Ms C.H., Nottinghamshire

Dear Ms C.H.,

Economics doctoral student Hugo Mialon argues that you need to analyse this as a two-player signalling game. You have two choices – fake or be honest about the earth's failure to move.

(Mialon comments helpfully, 'Faking is the strategy of a devoted girlfriend or courtesan, depending on whether the intent is to spare feelings or gain favours.') When you appear to be enjoying yourself, your partner also has two choices: to believe you or not.

The strategy Mialon advises depends on the intensity of your love, and on how likely you are to be enjoying yourself anyway, which in his model is a function of your age. His conclusion: the more you love your partner, and the further you are from thirty (the age at which your partner expects your capacity for orgasm to be greatest), the more you should fake.

I have to confess I found it all extremely complicated. I discussed it with my wife, but that didn't seem to help anybody very much. Yet several of Mialon's ideas have been supported by data from the 2000 Orgasm Survey. (Presumably, the name is chronological rather than quantitative.)

After much reflection I finally located my doubts: in Mialon's model, orgasms themselves are exogenous. The players cannot simply try a bit harder. This is an important omission, since one of the main arguments against faking is that it denies your partner the feedback he needs to improve.

Therefore I have decided to construct my own economic model of the subject. Meanwhile my advice is to stop faking orgasms and instead make sure your partner doesn't fake his foreplay.

Yours energetically, The Undercover Economist

Dear Undercover Economist,

I've been seeing my girlfriend for the past three years, and we've been living together for the past eighteen months. I just can't decide whether to propose to her this Valentine's Day or wait until next year. What would you suggest?

– Mr C. Johnson, Bristol

Dear Mr Johnson,

Evidently you intend to marry this lucky girl eventually, since your question implies that whether you propose now or later, the expected net present value created will be positive.

As the poet Andrew Marvell once explained, value-creating moves usually should be made sooner, rather than later, since time's winged chariot hurries near. But Marvell failed to anticipate advances in real option theory which demonstrate that it can be worth delaying decisions to obtain more information. You need to weigh up the cost of delay against the value of waiting to gain new information.

The cost of delay is small if you are young and patient. The value of waiting is large if you have the kind of exciting relationship where every day you learn something new about your belle. This is why young people are often counselled against rash betrothals.

On the other hand, you've been living with the girl for a while. Perhaps another year is unlikely to bring important information. If so, what are you waiting for? This reasoning has served your correspondent very well.

There is another important consideration: the window of opportunity for exercising an option can slam shut, in which case the option value is zero. There is no point learning everything you need to know to propose, if on Valentine's Day next year your girlfriend is dating somebody else. Before you decide to wait another year, it might be wise to be sure that she will wait too.

Yours in haste, The Undercover Economist

Dear Undercover Economist,

I seem to have a thing about young women. I will not see forty again, and while my friends (the female ones, admittedly) insist that I should be dating sophisticated thirty-something women with the aim of settling down, I find myself attracted to wild, volatile hellraisers. There has been Kristen, eighteen, catwalk model; Irene, twenty-two, Swedish law student; Janine, twenty, French heiress; and, most recently, Fleur, twenty-three, polo player (my God). My friends tell me my later years will be lonely, barren and desperate. Is it worth it?

– H. Humbert, London

Dear Mr Humbert,

Contrary to popular belief, economists have an optimistic disposition. We believe that when individuals are free to choose, they find life is full of mutually beneficial interactions, such as the ones you and Fleur enjoy. We also believe that just because something is fun doesn't mean it cannot last.

The contrary view – the view your friends hold – is that you need to drop Fleur like a hot potato and find yourself a member of the Bridget Jones generation. There are two possible reasons. First, perhaps women, like wine, improve with age. Your friends may believe this but when it comes to your happiness, your own preferences must be sovereign. Second, perhaps it is worth giving up your playboy lifestyle now to avoid loneliness later.

But I believe that your friends are giving you bad advice because they are jealous. Given that you are already successfully dating people half your age, why will this suddenly stop? Even if your hellraisers grow tired of you, you may then find that single women of a certain age are a renewable resource. But the most important reason for advising you to stick to girls is my own conscience: I am not sure the sophisticated women of the world could bear to experience your charms just yet.

Yours enviously, The Undercover Economist

Dear Undercover Economist,

I believe that there is an inexplicable shortage of sex. Given that studies show that women and men enjoy it more than most other activities, and given its intrinsically low cost, it appears that even a crude approximation of a utility-maximising person would probably spend much more time having sex than most. Do you know of any economic discussion of this?

– Michael Vassar, New York

Dear Michael,

It is true that there is something puzzling about the lack of sex in the world. Everybody says they enjoy sex, you can do it fairly safely for the price of a condom, and all you need is somebody of the appropriate gender and sexual preference. How difficult can it be?

Economics professor and blogger Tyler Cowen has offered an embarrassment of possible explanations. In the spirit of perfect competition between economic pundits I suggest that you need fewer answers.

We need just two complementary theories, one to explain the all-night-long sex that couples aren't having as much of as they should; and the other to explain the casual sex that strangers should be having with each other, and aren't.

For couples it's surely a case of diminishing returns. Just because the average utility of sex is high, doesn't mean that the marginal utility of more sex is also high.

I enjoy sex but I am no longer a teenager and, to be blunt, it takes me days to reload.

For strangers the risk of rejection, violence or social condemnation seems very high. In groups where these risks are lower (gay men, students, hippies), my theory predicts that more sex should be going on.

There is a simpler explanation, though: everybody is having constant, guilt-free sex. They just haven't told the economists.

Yours in curiosity, The Undercover Economist

Dear Undercover Economist,

I'm struggling with the dating game. I am told that one of the 'rules' is that I shouldn't accept a date for Saturday night unless I'm asked out by Wednesday at the latest. The idea, apparently, is to give the impression that I'm busy. Needless to say, I've missed out on the last three potential dates. Is this rule really wise?

– Bridget, London

Dear Bridget,

You have the right rule but the wrong explanation. You think that the rule is designed to signal unavailability. However, any game theorist will tell you that a credible signal has to be prohibitively costly to fake. This would be the case if only genuinely busy girls were able to refuse last-minute dates. If a signal can be easily faked it's not much of a signal, and since any wallflower can pretend to be busy, the signalling value of such pretence is zero because no man will pay attention to it.

The true role of the rule is not signalling but screening. The 'no last-minute dates' rule automatically disqualifies any man who is inconsiderate, short-sighted or just not particularly into you. The Nobel Prize-winning screening theory recognises the fact that without some foolproof system, women are incapable of telling a Mark Darcy from a Daniel Cleaver.

Admittedly, since you are ruling out dates with all the cads, the number of first dates you accept will fall – perhaps precipitously, depending on the proportion of playboys in your orbit. But the dates you do have will be quality-controlled: you will cut out all that unnecessary flirting, dressing up and snogging in the car at the end of the date, and replace it with long, steady relationships with reliable men. This is what you want, isn't it?

Dear Undercover Economist,

I'm busy and I'm looking for love, so I've posted my profile on some online dating sites. I make a good living in the City but, as I'm slightly overweight and my nose is too big, I've avoided including a photograph. So far I've not had a single reply – what am I doing wrong?

– Samantha Williamson, Shoreditch

Dear Samantha,

You can claim what you like and post a photo of a slim, stunning young model but, although such lies will secure you many enquiries, none of the dates are likely to go well. An optimum strategy is to go for mild exaggeration.

This is indeed what most people do, according to the economists Ali Hortacsu and Gunter Hitsch and the economic psychologist Dan Ariely. They studied thirty thousand online adverts to see what people were saying about themselves and whether it attracted replies.

People claim to be richer, slimmer, blonder and more beautiful than one would expect: two-thirds of online daters have 'above average' looks and just one in a hundred admit 'below average'. So, claim above-average looks yourself, and who is to gainsay you?

It may also be a mistake to be too candid about your high salary. Women reply to rich men but, for some reason, men prefer women with middling incomes.

Your biggest mistake, though, is not to post your photograph. People without photos rarely get enquiries – with good reason. Anyone with above-average looks will post a photo and prove it; those without photos, therefore, will be assumed to be plain. But then, those who are merely plain can also post photos. Then, those who are ugly will follow suit to distinguish themselves from those who shatter the camera lens. You don't want to bracket yourself down there, so point your sneezer at the camera and smile.

Above-averagely yours, The Undercover Economist

Dear Undercover Economist,

My boyfriend and I have always practised safe sex, but now we're talking about using just the pill rather than condoms. What concerns me is the risk of catching something. I expect my boyfriend slept with other girls before we started dating, but I feel fairly sure that he wouldn't have done anything risky.

Am I right?

– Cecilia Larson, Bristol

PS My boyfriend is an economist.

Dear Cecilia,

Oh dear. It was all looking so promising. Unprotected sex produces a classic negative externality. Someone who decides to have unsafe sex gets to enjoy all the pleasure but only part of the risk: if he contracts an infection, he will suffer from it himself but also risk passing it on to his future partners, and their partners' partners. The only reason you have been using condoms at all is that you know other people haven't bothered.

Your boyfriend knows this perfectly well. He may also know that some sexually transmitted diseases, such as chlamydia, have more serious effects in women than in men. Unsafe sex has benefits as well as risks; as an economist, he may well have decided that the personal risks are worth running.

Do not lose hope, though.

As a rational being, your boyfriend will have avoided the most unsafe practices, such as sharing needles and having unprotected intercourse with sex professionals. So your main risk is that he has had unprotected sex with a large number of ordinary women like you. But how likely is this? Such delights are likely to lie well outside his feasible consumption set: there is not usually a queue to jump into bed with economists.

Yours, playing it safe, The Undercover Economist

Dear Undercover Economist,

After several years I recently noted that I only really fancy my girlfriend after I've had a few drinks. Is this relationship worth pursuing?

– David Pigeon, London

Dear David,

I know how you feel: I only fancy chips when they're served with mayonnaise. Sadly for my waistline, my relationship with chips has not suffered.

You are saying that like chips and mayonnaise, alcohol and your girlfriend are complementary goods. I am not sure this is a problem.

It might be a problem if your predicament were unusual. It is not. Many people have found that alcohol has aphrodisiac qualities, even if it occasionally dampens the ability to follow through. This Christmas thousands of couples like you and your girlfriend will rediscover each other with the help of the Yuletide brandy. I'm a September baby myself, as is my father, my sister, her husband and their son. You are not alone!

Of course, it is easy to drink more alcohol than is good for you. Perhaps this is what is concerning you, but there seems to be no need for worry. The Government advises that the average man should aim to drink no more than three to four 'units' of alcohol – about two pints of ordinary-strength lager – a day. Since the typical British couple claims to make love every three days or so, you should be able to lubricate yourself appropriately without putting too much strain on your liver. Just steer clear of prodigious feats of love.

It seems to me that there is one cause for concern: your

girlfriend must never suspect that you need to don the beer goggles to find her appealing. Drinking is commonplace in our culture, so you shouldn't find it hard to camouflage the limits of your infatuation. Just don't do anything stupid, such as discussing it in the pages of a national newspaper.

Yours tipsily, The Undercover Economist

Dear Undercover Economist,

I think I'm a likeable person but I struggle to get dates. I've been told I give a bad first impression and just need to persuade women to get to know me a bit better. Some friends are dragging me to speed-dating but I can't see how a series of three-minute conversations can be anything other than a disaster. How I can persuade the girls to give me a second chance?

– James Atkinson, Clapham

Dear James,

Many people suffer from this problem – and not just people, but products too. Imagine a new manufacturer trying to persuade sceptical customers that a new DVD player is reliable. Nobody's ever heard of the company name, so how do they know the DVD player isn't going to break down after a few weeks?

The solution is for the company to offer money-back

guarantees offering to replace the player or refund the customer's money if the thing breaks within, say, three years. That gives the customer some insurance, but more importantly it's an unmistakable signal of the manufacturer's confidence in the product.

People who make poor-quality merchandise can't afford to promise to fix it.

You, too, need to offer a money-back guarantee. Go to the speed-dating session with two tickets for a top West End show and give them to a girl you like. Tell her that you are sure she will like you if she gets to know you, and that you suggest that she uses the tickets to take you on your third date. That's a measure of your confidence that she will want a third date. If not, she is free to take someone else.

I think this should work. It will certainly ensure that for the lucky lady, you will give a first impression that lasts.

Yours speedily, The Undercover Economist

Dear Undercover Economist,

My work recently took me to New York, where it kept me until Saturday morning. I invited my girlfriend to visit so we could spend the evening there together. As we split most big costs in our relationship, I proposed we share the cost of the hotel room and she cover her air fare. She argued that because my company had covered my air fare, I should split hers with her. I countered that either the utility of spending a nice evening in the city (during which I would have undoubtedly picked up dinner and the rest of the evening) was worth it to her, or it wasn't. Who is right?

– John Wegman, by email

Dear John,

You have thought about this problem in entirely the wrong way. Both you and your girlfriend have a case, but this disagreement is part of a much wider game.

Your trip has created joint gains for the pair of you and you are arguing over how to divide the spoils. There is no right way to do this. Your admission that you would pay for dinner and entertainment, although you normally split major costs, is an admission that the merits of the case are vague.

You might think that some fancy economic theorem will give you a precise answer. Nothing could be further from the truth. You will have such arguments many times, and game theory shows that in an indefinitely repeated game there are many possible outcomes, some good and some bad. The best are co-operative and profitable for both players – which suggests a little generosity on your part may go a long way.

Of course, you have everything to gain from penny-pinching if your relationship with your girlfriend is short-lived. You are going the right way about it.

Yours repetitively, The Undercover Economist

Dear Undercover Economist,

Bikini waxes: boyfriends seem to like the results, but they hurt. What would you say were the costs and benefits?

– Sylvia, via email

Dear Sylvia,

Thank you for sharing your concerns. I have never had a bikini wax myself and prefer not to comment on the aesthetic qualities of the practice. Nevertheless I believe there is an important economic insight to take on board: you are making what economists would call a 'relationship-specific investment', and such investments have consequences.

Admittedly getting a bikini wax is not as serious a business as having a child or a prominent tattoo reading 'Sylvia for Tim'. But it is something that only one boyfriend is likely to enjoy; should he prove insufficiently appreciative, it is not something you can advertise to other admirers unless you have a very frank flirtation technique.

When businesses install equipment to satisfy a particular customer they usually do so only when protected by cost-sharing arrangements or a long-term contract; sometimes the client will even merge with its supplier. Those who do not, risk being exploited: once the one-sided commitment has been made and the costs have been sunk, they find the other side reneging on the deal.

For you, cost-sharing might be a fancy weekend away; a long-term contract might specify that your boyfriend does the washing up.

And as for a merger? Marriage, of course, or an engagement assured by a suitably expensive rock.

Whatever you want from your boyfriend, make sure you get it before making your own painful investment. You need to understand when your bargaining power is waning or – ahem – waxing.

Yours baldly, The Undercover Economist

Dear Undercover Economist,

Traditionally women have to wait for men to propose marriage – or indeed a date. Isn't this out of date and unfair, too?

– Fiona O'Callaghan, Dublin

Dear Fiona,

It has been out of date since 1962, when David Gale and Lloyd Shapley published a paper on the problem of who marries whom, to work out whether there is a way of pairing up men and women so that no potential adulterers would rather marry each other. There may be loveless singletons around, but as long as nobody wants to marry them, the situation is said to be a 'stable assignment'.

Gale and Shapley suggested an algorithm guaranteed to produce a stable assignment. Each man proposed to his preferred partner; each woman then rejected all the less attractive offers and kept the remaining fellow on tenterhooks in case someone better came along. The rejects would then propose marriage to someone closer to their league, each woman would reject all but the best so far, and the humiliating process would continue.

The algorithm eventually produces a stable assignment, where nobody prefers a willing partner to the one they have. It also produces a billion broken hearts; presumably the assignment is stable because nobody wants to go through the whole thing again.

The algorithm works equally well if the women do the proposing and the men do the rejecting. Intuitively it's not clear which you should prefer, but the mathematics are unambiguous: out of all the stable assignments that exist, the one where men propose is the very worst for women and the very best for men. Nearly five decades after this revelation a change in tradition is probably overdue.

Stably yours, The Undercover Economist

Dear Undercover Economist,

I have been going out with a schoolfriend for nearly a year and I think he's 'the one' – but we are heading off to university at opposite ends of the country. Will the relationship survive? Is there anything I can do to keep it going?

– Natasha, County Durham

Dear Natasha,

I understand your concern, but your future looks bright. A long-distance relationship will always put pressure on both of you, but it's a question of how you use that to your advantage.

Economist Tyler Cowen, of George Mason University, has pointed out that the Alchian-Allen Theorem applies to any long-distance relationship.

The theorem, briefly, implies that Australians drink higher-quality Californian wine than Californians, and vice-versa, because it is only worth the transportation costs for the most expensive wine. Similarly there is no point in travelling to see your boyfriend for a take-away Indian meal and an evening in front of the telly. To justify the trip's fixed costs you will require champagne, sparkling conversation and energetic sex. Insist on it.

Meanwhile optimal-experimentation theory suggests that at this tender stage of life you are highly likely to meet someone even better. Socialise a lot while your boyfriend is not around.

Finally consider your bargaining strength with potential new boyfriends with regard to, for instance, who pays for dinner. Your best alternative to a negotiated agreement with the new boyfriend is your old boyfriend, who by your admission is an excellent catch.

This puts you in a sound negotiating position – unless, of course, the boy is maintaining a long-distance relationship of his own.

Yours from a distance, The Undercover Economist

———

Dear Undercover Economist,

I've fallen in love with my best friend. Whenever we go out we have the best of times but, for a reason I seem unable to comprehend, she has not clearly indicated that she feels the same for me as I do for her. I see a risk of alienating her as a friend if I tell her how I feel for her. Quite an exposure in my view.

Any suggestions?

– F, Austria

Dear F,

Economics now devotes much attention to the study of knowledge, and economists distinguish between 'mutual knowledge' – you know you love her and she knows you love her, but you do not know that she knows – and 'common knowledge', where you know that she knows that you know that . . . ad infinitum.

The distinction might seem over-fine, but in your case it may be critical. The most likely scenario, frankly, is that your friend can read you like a book but prefers to ignore your crush. The ambiguity of mere mutual knowledge preserves your friendship, but a declaration of love would create common knowledge and doom it.

The alternative possibility is the one you hope for: she loves you but does not know of your love. You need to discover whether this is true without risking all, so simply ask a friend of hers to make enquiries.

Another option, of course, is to write a letter to the *FT*. If your friend is pretending not to notice your ardour she can also pretend not to notice your letter. The fatal transparency of common knowledge is avoided and your friendship can continue.

If by some miracle she loves you but is blind to your feelings, your letter will solve this problem. Fingers crossed for the next few days, eh?

Yours transparently, The Undercover Economist

Dear Undercover Economist,

I'm looking for 'the one'. Is he out there?

– Ruth, Barcelona

Dear Ruth,

It might help if we understand which elements of marriage are common to many potential husbands, and which are unique to 'the one'.

First, marriage offers economies of scale in production, particularly production of children. Husband and wife can each specialise in different skills, according to their comparative advantage. I fail to see why you cannot realise these economies of scale with almost anyone. Second, there are economies of scale in consumption. One garden will do, so will one kitchen.

The real question, then, is whether you can stand the person you marry enough to enjoy these efficiencies. Here economics had little to say until a recent breakthrough by the economists Michèle Belot and Marco Francesconi. They examined data from a speed-dating company, and discovered, unsurprisingly, that women like tall, rich, well-educated men. Men like slim, educated women who do not smoke.

The more intriguing finding emerged when pickings were scarce. Women 'ticked' about 10 per cent of men as worthy of further investigation, regardless of the quality of a particular crop. If the men were short and poor, then the women lowered their standards and still picked 10 per cent. The men, too, abandoned unrealistic ambitions. They 'ticked' about a quarter of the women, regardless of quality. This happened even though each could have a complimentary speed-date another time if he or she found no one they liked.

My conclusion: even when there is little to be lost from maintaining standards, people are very quick to lower them. My advice: do likewise.

Yours pragmatically, The Undercover Economist

Dear Undercover Economist,

Following the sudden and unexpected cessation of romance with a sustainable economic development researcher, am I due any recompense for giving up Christmas with my family and investing emotionally and financially in both a transatlantic flight and eleven of my twenty days of annual leave, given that there was the suggestion that 'next year we can spend it with your family' or indeed that there would be a next year at all?

– Sophie, London

Dear Sophie,

Oh dear. You appear to have fallen for a variant of the oldest trick in the book: the promise that he will still respect you in the morning. Clearly you are deserving of compensation, but that is hardly the point. The question is whether there is any prospect of you receiving it.

Life is full of situations in which we are asked to bear a cost today in exchange for a benefit later – salaries are typically paid in arrears, for example. We put up with the risk because we are relying on the reputation of the person or company we're dealing with, usually backed by the courts.

If that reputation is worthless – say, he is a 'sustainable economic development researcher' – then the courts will have to do. In 1920s America courts would enforce 'breach of promise' suits for ladies who had been promised marriage, slept with the cad and then been dumped – a situation not dissimilar to yours. Courts no longer do this, which is why it became traditional to supplement such proposals with non-refundable deposits, to be worn on the ring finger.

If you happen to have such a deposit, all is well. Otherwise all you have received for your pains is a valuable lesson.

Yours faithlessly, The Undercover Economist

Dear Undercover Economist,

I am thirty-eight years old, rather bored with my husband, and for the past two months I have been flirting like mad with another man. We often meet

up for a drink and the talk has started to get quite
saucy. I'm sure I could take things further if I wanted.
Should I?

– Sheila, London

Dear Sheila,

When I heard of your dilemma I thought immediately of an old
paper from the *Journal of Political Economy*, 'A Theory of Extramarital Affairs' by Ray C. Fair, an economist at Yale.

Professor Fair modelled affairs as a time-allocation problem.
That seems odd. But on reflection Professor Fair's approach may
have been perceptive: I suspect that affairs do take up a lot of
time and that this mundane fact looms large in most adulterers'
lives.

That said, his approach to the problem could equally have
applied if you had written to say that you were thirty-eight
years old, rather bored with your husband and were thinking of
taking up badminton. One senses that something is missing. I
think the omission is uncertainty. You do not know how much
fun an affair will be. Nor do you know whether your husband is
likely to become more or less tedious over time. A cost-benefit
analysis is going to be tricky, but we can say for sure that your
potential affair represents a valuable option. As with all options
it may be best to refrain from exercising it until the option is
'deep in the money' – that is, until you are so thoroughly fed up
with your husband that you think nothing can save the
marriage.

Until then why not enjoy the saucy talk? It may be a lot more
fun than the affair itself.

Yours busily, The Undercover Economist

Dear Undercover Economist,

I am seventeen years old and studying A-level economics.

A lot of my friends are getting into serious relationships and I'd like to get a girlfriend myself, but I am also concerned about getting distracted from my studies. How does the cost-benefit analysis work out?

– Ben, Buckinghamshire

Dear Ben,

A lot of economists have been arguing about this. Social conservatives have recently argued that 'abstinence until marriage builds character and self-control'.

More plausibly, as the economist Joseph Sabia suggests in a forthcoming article, 'If the realised benefits of sexual intercourse are higher than the ex ante anticipated benefits, adolescents may substitute time and energy away from investments in human capital and towards investments in future obtainment of sex.'

In English that means that sex may be distracting because it is surprisingly fun.

There is little doubt that virgins achieve better grades. Yet is this because sex kills brain cells or because kids who are already bored at school look harder for ways to amuse themselves? Professor Sabia's article in *Economic Inquiry* uses data on the timing of the decision to have sex to show that kids who decide to have sex were already doing badly at school.

Professor Sabia's results show that a girl does not seem to be distracted at all by losing her virginity – perhaps because young boyfriends are not competent enough to be terribly distracting.

Be careful, though, because it's different for boys. Professor Sabia finds that deciding to have sex will knock a few percentage points off your grade. That's my excuse for doing so badly at maths and I'm sticking to it.

Yours distractedly, The Undercover Economist

Dear Undercover Economist,

I have just joined a dating website in the hope of finding true love. Friends of mine have started dating someone they met online, only for a 'better offer' to arise on the website. If this happens what should I do?

– Duncan, London

Dear Duncan,

The possibility of upgrading to a better relationship is not new, but internet dating allows more offers to be considered and so the tried-and-tested rules of thumb may no longer be appropriate.

It might seem natural simply to consider how many offers you must sample until you are likely to meet 'Ms Right'. That would be naive. You must instead balance the benefits of choice against the effect your flightiness may have on your targets.

These decisions are much like those faced by a company choosing the optimal number of suppliers. Dealing with more suppliers allows the company to choose the cheapest and best. But having too many makes suppliers insecure and unwilling to invest in the relationship.

Your ideal choice depends on what you want. Fun and frolics are ideally obtained by keeping options open, perhaps even switching to the spot market. But if you want your partner to have your babies, support you while you write your novel or share the cost of buying a home, you will need to reassure her that you do not have other competitors waiting in the wings.

In some industries it is common to sign contracts with two suppliers – enough competition to keep each on its toes but enough commitment to inspire big investment in the relationship. In your case that would be a wife and a long-term mistress. Perhaps the tried-and-tested rules of thumb work after all.

Yours optimally, The Undercover Economist

Dear Undercover Economist,

I've been dating someone for a few months and the relationship is now quite serious. There's just one problem: his dog. I've no strong feelings about dogs, but he's had this mutt for years and seems to love it more than he loves me. I could swallow my reservations and see where the relationship goes or I could opt for the old 'either the dog goes or I do' ultimatum. What should I do?

– Canophobic in Kettering

Dear Canophobic,

The news isn't good. The evidence – gathered from twenty years of data by the economists Peter Schwarz, Jennifer Troyer and Jennifer Beck Walker – suggests that the pooch may indeed dog your relationship.

Your letter does not mention whether you want to have children, but if you do the dog is a problem. Households with young children tend not to own dogs – suggesting that the dog is a good substitute for a baby. Or to flip it around, households with dogs tend not to have young children.

If you get over that hump, when the kids are older your family is more likely to want a dog. By then, though, this one will probably have breathed his last. So it's not just this dog but dogs from here to eternity.

Worse yet, the figures show that when households earn more money the women tend to want to spend it on the children and the men tend to spend it on pets. (Think of the dog as a supertoy, like a motorbike or a fancy piece of hi-fi.) Only poverty, it seems, can save you from bitter arguments over how to spend money.

So by all means tell him it's you or the dog. But please don't expect to get the answer you hope for.

Yours doggedly, The Undercover Economist

Dear Undercover Economist,

I am worried that if my children receive sex education at school it will make unwanted pregnancies more likely. Should I take them out of class?

– Protective Parent

Dear Protective Parent,

You are right to be worried. It is easy to see why information about contraception might encourage sex by lowering its costs, but the effects might be more dramatic than you would think. In a nutshell fixed costs are your problem. These are obvious when it comes to, for instance, producing software. The first copy may cost hundreds of millions of dollars to produce, the second very little. But losing your virginity is like that too: the first sexual experience comes with a psychological cost, but, once paid, future experiences are easier. (Economics students will recognise the implication: sex has economies of scale, so it is efficient to have either lots or none at all.)

Within a relationship, too, the first sexual experience probably has a fixed cost.

In both cases access to contraceptives makes it likelier that the first experience will be chosen; having crossed that barrier, it may become so attractive to have sex that teenagers will do so even when the contraceptives are not available.

The economists Peter Arcidiacono and Ahmed Khwaja, of Duke University, with Lijing Ouyang of the US Centers for Disease Control and Prevention, believe that this is the way teenagers do indeed behave.

Yet I would not advise you to shield your children from sex education. That might be wise if prevention of pregnancy and disease were your goals, but that is too extreme. Your children will know that sex has benefits as well as costs. Perhaps you should refresh your memory about these?

Yours educatedly, The Undercover Economist

Dear Undercover Economist,

I am a woman in my early thirties. I am also a virgin. Should I be?

– Gloria, New York

Dear Gloria,

Let me lay out the relevant economic theory and evidence. Theory first: economists have often theorised that women should have evolved preferences to be more careful than men about whom they have sex with. The basic reasoning is that it takes a woman nine months to produce a baby while it takes a man about ninety seconds. However, birth control is much better than it was in the environment in which these preferences evolved. Perhaps, then, your preferences are more cautious than they should be.

What about the evidence? The economist Alan Collins, in a paper titled 'Surrender Value of Capital Assets: The Economics of Strategic Virginity Loss', assesses whether men and women lose their virginity in different circumstances. The key conclusion is that almost 60 per cent of women say they lost their virginity because they were in love; just over 35 per cent of men offered this reason. Collins believes this supports the socio-biological view that women are making an investment when they lose their virginity and so need to choose their partners with care. Men are simply engaging in consumption – that is, having fun.

Collins also discovers that people who found out about sex by talking with friends (rather than, for instance, from books) were more likely to lose their virginity for non-romantic reasons. Perhaps they wanted something to talk about. I suggest that you get some friends over for a girly chat about the facts of life. All investments should begin with research.

Yours non-romantically, The Undercover Economist

Dear Undercover Economist,

I am seventeen years old and my school only recently became coeducational. The other sixth-form students are almost all male, like me. I feel that the school does not meet my romantic needs and that I will never know true love while at school. In fact I'm not having much luck at finding any love at all. Please can you help or even just offer some hope?

– Truly Lovelorn Student K, Bedford

Dear Student K,

You are right. The sixth form does not meet your romantic needs. Even if the boys only mildly outnumbered the girls – say, fifty-five to forty-five – then assuming everyone paired off in the traditional fashion there would be ten boys left out, hormones raging, willing to offer the girls a better deal in one way or another. Sensible girls know how to exploit this healthy competition in their favour.

Still, as you grow older, your time will come. In cities across the developed world dating-age women outnumber dating-age men. (Economist Lena Edlund argues that women have more to gain from city life than men.)

The excess supply of datable women and the resulting dating disadvantage forces women into bursts of self-improvement, which may explain why they tend to be better dressed and better educated than men. Research by economists Kerwin Charles and Ming Luoh finds a similar effect when many otherwise-marriageable men end up in prison. It does not take much to tip a dating market out of equilibrium and your plight seems particularly extreme.

Yet take heart. At your age I was in an even worse situation at an all-boys school. All seemed lost until I discovered that the girls' school opposite was willing to look for some gains from trade.

Yours, in excess supply, The Undercover Economist

Dear Undercover Economist,

I have fallen in love with a wonderful man and on Valentine's Day he proposed to me. We're planning to marry next summer. The question is: should we live together over the next year or wait until we're married? The financial impact is relatively small either way and I am not afraid of scandal. I am just trying to work out whether some time living together is likely to make our marriage stronger or not.

– Elspeth, Boston, MA

Dear Elspeth,

For many years theory pointed in one direction and evidence in the other. The theory – going back to Nobel laureate Gary Becker's work in the 1970s – is that a period of cohabitation lets you learn more about one another and thus avoid a bad match. Your man may be charming on a date but if he leaves his underpants lying around or eats toast over the sink to save washing up, forget it.

The overwhelming evidence, on the other hand, used to be that marriages preceded by cohabitation were more likely to break down – in the US at least. The question is whether this was a causal relationship or whether the cohabitation and the marital breakdown were caused by a third factor, such as social class or a lack of religious belief.

Fortunately new empirical research from economist Steffen Reinhold suggests both that the relationship between cohabitation and divorce is not causal and that it has faded over time as more educated, middle-class couples choose to live together before marriage.

I recommend following Becker's theory: learn about the marriage before it is too late by moving in together now. Keep an eye out for discarded underpants.

Yours forewarned, The Undercover Economist

Dear Undercover Economist,

I am about to be married and have no doubts about the relationship. But there is one nagging worry: my fiancé co-owns a condo overlooking the Pacific Ocean near San Francisco – with an ex-girlfriend who lives next door to it. She is not in a position to buy him out of his investment and, although they rent it out, the mortgage is steep. I believe the condo is an investment specific to the former relationship and would like it divested – but the housing market is a shambles.

– Mary, USA

Dear Mary,

While I sympathise with your problem, I must correct you. A relationship-specific investment is one that is worth more within a relationship than outside it, such as a set of wedding photos. The condo is not relationship-specific, just unprofitable and il-liquid.

The condo can therefore be disposed of without destroying value – but not, it seems, by either side buying the other side out.

If your fiancé sold his share to a stranger, he'd sell at a loss. But in truth the loss has already happened; his reluctance to sell suggests he's pig-headed as well as an incompetent investor.

So I recommend that you buy out your fiancé's share at a fire-sale price. Subsequent negotiations about the condo would then be between you and the ex. Should your marriage work out you can share the profits with your fiancé. And if not at least you will have prearranged some compensation.

Yours profitably, The Undercover Economist

I work as an escort in Canary Wharf, one of London's financial centres. I wonder if you might have some sound business advice on how workers in my industry should tackle the sudden drop in demand following the collapse of Lehman Brothers in September 2008?

– Miss C

Dear Miss C,

I wasn't aware that escort services were pro-cyclical but I shall take your word for it. You have three options, none of them perfect.

One: relocate. Canary Wharf is a pure banking play and you could seek a more diversified market. The West End is full of hedge funds, oil barons and old money. However, I recognise that it will take some effort to find new clients. The economist Steve Levitt and sociologist Sudhir Venkatesh discovered, in a recent analysis of Chicago street prostitution, that the industry was very concentrated because prostitutes and clients would otherwise fail to find each other. You, of course, are not in quite the same game and may be able to relocate with ease.

Two: tough it out at Canary Wharf and hope that supply falls to match demand. Levitt and Venkatesh found that the supply of street prostitution was highly elastic in response to a demand surge. (The fourth of July holiday provokes a spike in trade for prostitutes – who knew?) Existing prostitutes would work longer hours, other prostitutes would travel to the area, and women who didn't normally work as prostitutes at all would dabble in the business. This suggests that many of your rivals will find something else to do in the tough times.

Three: you may find that escort services are a little like estate agency, in that even severe demand shocks don't tend to reduce fees. You'd find yourself well paid when in work but frequently idle. That spare time could be used to study or find a part-time sideline.

I would give exactly the same advice to an estate agent.

Yours elastically, The Undercover Economist

How to Spend Your Lottery Win
Work, School and Money

Whether at school or as part of a career, work dominates our time, determines our moods and even defines our identity. When we meet someone new our first serious question is rarely 'Are you married?' or 'What are your hobbies?', but 'What do you do?'. The answer we give to that question not only defines us in the eyes of others but shapes our self-image. No wonder we economists are so keen to stress that our subject offers insights into realms other than mundane financial bean-counting.

Indeed economists tend to be unexpectedly indifferent to matters of money. It is a complicating superficial distraction that can usually be assumed away without much harm being done. It may be natural to look to economics for guidance about earnings but I rarely give purely financial advice. I am more fascinated by the deeper-running currents of the working environment: office politics, truth and lies, power and promotion.

This section of correspondence applies free-market principles to diary planning and asks what the theory of comparative advantage has to say about the ultimate career question: should I chase the money or follow my dreams? It advises a lottery winner who doesn't trust herself to spend her windfall wisely. And it addresses the age-old question of whether money can buy you happiness, now the subject of intense study by 'happiness economists'. The short answer: of course it can but don't expect it to come cheap.

Dear Undercover Economist,

I leave university this summer and have been applying
for jobs with some of the big banks and consulting
firms. I've received a couple of offers but they will
be withdrawn if I don't respond within ten days. These
are good jobs and I'd hate to lose the offers but
I'd also like to see what else is around. What should
I do?

– Suzanne Smith, Cambridge

Dear Ms Smith,

Many companies try the 'exploding offer' trick. Some career
advisers say you shouldn't work for any company whose human
resources department behaves like that. This reasoning makes
sense only if you assume that the HR department is rep-
resentative of the company as a whole – thankfully it often is
not.

Game theory, which looks at the later moves of a game and
reasons backwards from that point, will give you more solid
career advice. A small company hiring only one candidate may
have a legitimate reason to require a quick decision but larger
firms are playing games. It is not to their advantage to withdraw
the offer because if you were a desirable recruit in January you
will still be a desirable recruit in June.

A company might try to make these threats more credible by
making them a matter of strict policy. However, graduates who
are bullied into accepting send a signal that they are not

confident of getting other offers. And if top-quality candidates who delay accepting are turned down, the policy would lead to a poor class of recruits.

If you wait before accepting an 'exploding offer', you will either find that the threat was empty or that the offer is withdrawn, leading you to conclude that you didn't want the job anyway because all your colleagues would have been second-rate. Be courteous, refuse to be hurried, and watch what happens next.

Yours patiently, The Undercover Economist

Dear Undercover Economist,

I am studying economics. The examiners mark to a curve, giving the top grade to the best 10 per cent of students, the next grade to the next 20 per cent, and so on. If we can agree to slack off simultaneously, we can get the same marks as we would have if we'd worked flat-out. But organising this is easier said than done. Can you suggest anything?

– Andrew Spencer, 'Cantorbridge' College

Dear Andrew,

Obviously you are already slacking off, otherwise you would remember what cartel theory teaches about tacit collusion. Let me remind you.

In equilibrium each student works fairly hard and grades are determined by talent and appetite for work. You would all like to work less hard and get the same grades for less effort. However, this is not an equilibrium because each student has an incentive to swot a little in secret and secure a top grade without much effort.

To make the agreement stick, you need to increase the rewards for slacking (arrange events with cheap beer), reduce the benefits of hard work (force people to share findings, start a lecture rota so notes can be passed around and form revision groups to discourage solo studying) and punish swots.

Punishment is important. Turn swots into social pariahs; whenever someone is caught studying organise coordinated bursts of hard work, in which everybody suffers as their relative grades go nowhere but their absolute effort increases. Such tactics work best if you can observe each other: continuous assessment means you can identify swots early and take action to deter their zeal. Cheap beer, swapping notes and bullying diligent students shouldn't be beyond you: it seems to work for every other university.

Yours lazily, The Undercover Economist

Dear Undercover Economist,

I am an economics lecturer at a prestigious university. It is policy to grade students relative to each other rather than to any absolute standard. The trouble is, I suspect that they may all be trying to slack off simultaneously to enjoy the same grades without any hard work. My suspicions were further aroused by reading last week's 'Dear Economist', which appeared to have been written by said students. What should I do?

– Professor X, 'Cantorbridge' College

Dear Professor X,

Any attempt to organise a 'slackers' cartel' is likely to be undermined because each student will have an incentive to work a little harder in secret, enjoying high grades for little extra effort. The cartel will try to increase the pay-off to slacking and punish those who work. Your countermeasures must increase the pay-off to hard work and make punishment more difficult.

Start by refusing to give your students any interim grades or constructive comments. This will make it harder for them to identify anyone who is doing well. Omit important, easily monitorable information from your lectures and make sure it is accessible instead in obscure textbooks that can be read secretly. Make your reading lists inordinately long so that it is hard for students to check up on who is reading what.

Finally be sure to examine your students in a single set of colossal exams rather than through continuous assessment. Your slackers will find it hard to monitor who is cheating the cartel by working hard, and by the time they find out the course will be over and it will be too late.

If you, an economics lecturer, cannot outwit a student cartel, then they had little to learn from you in any case.

Yours, in an educational spirit, The Undercover Economist

Dear Undercover Economist,

I have a simple request. I just want to be happy. Can you help?

– Ms Jessica Granger, Kirkby Stephen

Dear Ms Granger,

This is hardly something to be ashamed of, and you have come to the right place for advice. Economists have been studying this subject intensively.

Nobel laureate Danny Kahneman asked a large sample of working women to describe what they had done and how they had felt throughout the previous day. If their experience is a guide, easily your best option is to have a lot of sex. Exercise, food, prayer and socialising also make people feel happy. Commuting makes people miserable. Any kind of human company is cheering, unless the other person is your boss. If you are having sex with your boss, Professor Kahneman's survey cannot offer advice.

But perhaps you need a more long-term view of life's choices. London School of Economics Professor Richard Layard recently surveyed the subject.

At first sight the insights are commonplace: money does buy some happiness while divorce and unemployment make you sad. To give an idea of the size of the effect, losing your job and a third of your income is four times more depressing than just losing the income. Getting divorced is nearly as bad; being separated but not divorced is even worse.

The advice is clear: first, don't make career choices that jeopardise your marriage; second, a secure job with moderate pay will make you happier than a shaky job with high pay.

Finally form low expectations. People with a high-earning peer group, women whose sisters marry rich men, and people with a lot of education but little income are all miserable. This may explain the sour demeanour of many journalists.

Yours joyfully, The Undercover Economist

Dear Undercover Economist,

At the end of each day my friend puts all his loose change into a large (empty) whisky bottle. After six months he banks three hundred pounds. This seems a good way of saving. What do you consider are the pros and cons of this method?

– Gordon Scripps, Cambridge

Dear Mr Scripps,

The advantages of your friend's approach are, at first sight, unclear. He frequently rids himself of loose change but by doing so ensures that every transaction generates yet more change. He also deprives himself of five pounds a year in interest.

Carrying a bottle of coins to the bank every six months seems more hassle than setting up a standing order into a savings account, but perhaps such a bottle on the mantelpiece is what passes for a conversation piece in Cambridge. Let us assume, therefore, that the excitement of such a savings method is adequate compensation both for the inconvenience and the lost interest.

Even then there is no obvious merit to this scheme. So my guess is that your friend values the way that saving appears painless. This is inexplicable behaviour according to the textbook, but the broad-minded economist Thomas Schelling would argue that your friend's behaviour is best explained by a split personality. Your friend wants to save on behalf of his long-term future self yet realises that this evening he will be a different person, blowing any loose change in the pub fruit machines.

The whisky bottle is a strategic commitment device in the three-player game between your friend this afternoon, your friend this evening and your friend in retirement. Unfortunately I don't think fifty pounds a month will provide much of a pension. I doubt that it will even pay for the psychiatrist.

Yours strategically, The Undercover Economist

Dear Undercover Economist,

My son has become addicted to economics. The more diligently I confiscate his economics books, the more he steals from my purse. I'm determined that he should grow up to be normal, frequenting the pub like everyone else. What should I do?

– Stymied in Stratford

Dear Stymied,

You tell a sad story but one that can be analysed using the theory of rational addiction developed by economists such as George Stigler, Gary Becker and Kevin Murphy.

Addictive goods and activities have some interesting properties. First, addictiveness itself: the pleasure produced by consumption is higher if past consumption has been high. In other words the more heroin, alcohol or neoclassical growth theory the addict has consumed, the less bearable it will be to abstain now.

Second, past consumption will also have a direct bearing on the addict's happiness. Typically we think of negative addictions: past consumption of crack makes for a miserable junkie today. But positive addictions are possible too. A progressive addiction to yoga or to reading may make for a happier and happier person. I am addicted to my wife – so far with unambiguously positive results.

Your son's addiction is probably a positive one, which will make him ever more fulfilled. But even if it is a negative addiction you must remember that rational addicts are utility maximisers. He may have been driven to addiction by circumstances – a desire to escape an over-controlling parent, for instance – but trying to frustrate his desires will make him more miserable.

What could be more heart-rending than to see a true passion for economics crushed by an economically illiterate parent?

I must urge you to stop your ill-advised policy of prohibition and adopt the more enlightened approach of laissez-faire.

Yours, from a pusher, The Undercover Economist

———————

Dear Undercover Economist,

I receive vastly more invitations to speak than I can manage. Some will be very lucrative, some will be very interesting and some will be easy to do. Many, however, will be neither lucrative nor interesting nor easy to do. Invitations start arriving up to a year and a half beforehand and then with increasing frequency almost right up to the last moment. What is the optimal response strategy, assuming that I never pull out of engagements once accepted?

– A Prominent Economist, London

Dear Sir or Madam,

Although you cannot guarantee that you will never regret accepting an invitation, you can optimise your diary simply enough.

First, combine ease, interest and your speaker's fee into a single measure of what makes an attractive invitation. If you later find yourself impoverished, overworked or under-stimulated, adjust that combination accordingly.

Then treat each slot on your calendar as a separate optimal experimentation problem. When an invitation arrives you will know from experience how attractive the invitation is and how many others are likely to materialise between now and the speaking date. If the answer is four, only accept an invitation that experience shows is in the top quartile: on balance it's likely to be the best you get. The closer you get to the speaking date, the lower you should set your standards for acceptance.

You should also maintain a 'reservation price' below which you prefer free time – especially, I suggest, on your wedding anniversary. If you anticipate becoming more popular, you will expect more attractive invitations in larger quantities and should set higher standards. The converse also applies – so beware cut-price competitors. There are some smart young economists around, you know.

Yours eloquently, The Undercover Economist

Dear Undercover Economist,

Will having more money make me happier?

– Karl Johnston, Glasgow

Dear Mr Johnston,

I have been asked the secret of happiness before but your question is rather specific. To answer it we need to turn to economist Andrew Oswald.

He has worked with numerous collaborators to calculate a 'happiness equation', based on analysing thousands of people's responses to questions about their contentment. His conclusion is that, assuming nothing else changes, more money makes them happier. He backs it up with a piece of work studying what happens to people who unexpectedly win lotteries – they, too, become happier.

This is what economists expect; not because we believe that people value money for its own sake but because money can buy all kinds of things, and if none of them brought you any pleasure you'd have to be an exceptionally incompetent shopper.

So the simple answer to your question is yes, more money will make you happier. But be careful – simply pursuing money will not, if your relationships, health or job security suffer. Oswald shows that these are vastly more important than money. Getting married produces £70,000-a-year's worth of joy, although given the cost of weddings these days that's not much of a bargain. Staying healthy and employed are more important still, worth tens of thousands of pounds a month.

Envy plays a sinister role. Oswald shows that happiness increases with higher income but it falls with higher expectations. The higher the income of your peer group the more depressed you tend to be. This is not good news for you: since you ask smart questions and read the *Financial Times*, you must expect a lot out of life. Oswald suggests that you are likely to be disappointed.

Yours contentedly, The Undercover Economist

Dear Undercover Economist,

My son-in-law has been unemployed for a couple of months now. As far as I can make out he's enjoying a PlayStation lifestyle while being supported by the state and by my daughter, who has had to find a temporary job. What concerns me is that he'll get used to this. Should I tell my daughter to apply pressure by quitting her job?

– Godfrey Pickens, Bedfordshire

Dear Mr Pickens,

The issue here is whether your son-in-law's preferences will change over time – will he 'get used' to a life of leisure and so be less likely to work?

There are two competing views here. One is that he will become hooked on leisure (the 'welfare trap' hypothesis) and will work less in future, even if his wife quits her job. The other, equally plausible in theory, is that he will become addicted to the extra income provided by his wife's new job and that if she quits he will go on to work harder than before.

Such competing hypotheses have been hard to test in the past. But economist John Kagel has succeeded in running a series of experiments that shed light on the matter. Kagel first forces his subjects to work for their income. Then for a while he provides them with a substantial unearned income – a kind of welfare, if you will.

Unsurprisingly they slack off at once. Later he withdraws the welfare and observes whether they work more or less than before welfare had ever been paid. The answer: it makes very little difference.

This implies that your wife should keep working for a while and see what happens. No harm will result. The only question for you is whether Kagel's findings apply to your son-in-law. Kagel's subjects were rats. Do you think the parallel with your son-in-law is close enough?

Yours experimentally, The Undercover Economist

Dear Undercover Economist,

I am seventeen and want to be a professional musician (I play the bass). My parents insist that I go to university to study music. Shouldn't I just get out there and play?

— Joanna Kay, Chicago

Dear Joanna,

Your decision chiefly depends on the returns to human capital versus the returns to alternative investments. The opportunity cost of going to college is that you could otherwise work, gain musical experience, and put the money you earn and the college fees you save into a diversified investment portfolio. If the expected income from the portfolio is lower than the expected increase in your earnings after the age of twenty-one, your parents are correct.

The returns to such straightforward financial investments are much lower than the human capital investment of going to college. So your parents would seem to have a strong argument, especially since partying and late-rising at college are often more fun than real work.

But let's not be hasty; a professional musician gets to go to a lot of parties, and different professions enjoy different returns to human capital investments. What, specifically, are the returns to education for musicians?

Thomas Smith of the University of Illinois, himself a jazz bassist, has examined the data on the earnings of jazz musicians. He's uncovered a surprising fact: while the returns to schooling are 10 per cent for classical or other non-jazz performances, they are actually negative for jazz performances.

In other words if you plan to play jazz, every year spent at school is a costly distraction. Professional playing experience, by contrast, is especially valuable for jazz musicians. Tell your parents to save their college fees and subsidise your first couple of years at the University of Life.

Yours tunefully, The Undercover Economist

Dear Undercover Economist,

Following the parable of the talents, my local church has handed out ten pounds to each of its churchgoers as 'seed money', which it hopes will multiply to raise funds for the church. What should I do with my ten pounds?

– H.T., London

Dear H.T.,

The parable tells of a master entrusting money to three slaves before departing on a long journey. Two of the slaves double the investment by the time he returns. Is this a parable about the virtues of stewardship or about eye-popping investment success? Your pastor is clearly salivating at the prospect of the latter, but he is being foolish.

The very phrase 'seed money' suggests venture capital and expectations of glorious growth.

I am sorry to awaken you rudely from this daydream but you have to remember that biblical Judaea was severely capital-constrained. Anyone lucky enough to have investment capital had a great choice of projects and 100 per cent returns were not uncommon. A comparable present-day return on your money might be 10 per cent, or a pound. Had Jesus wanted to deliver a parable about extraordinary investment savvy, he'd have said that the slaves quintupled the money.

Second, a 'talent' was worth £550 or more in today's money, the kind of sum that would fund participation in a significant venture. And third, household slaves were experienced money-managers. In contrast your church is dishing out peanuts to monkeys.

Most serious of all, the parable of the talents has a master entrusting money to slaves who could not run away. You, on the other hand, are a free agent.

I usually hesitate to proffer investment advice but, since you ask, there is nothing to constrain you from investing your ten pounds in a round of drinks.

Yours piously, The Undercover Economist

Dear Undercover Economist,

I am majoring in strategic and production management at a German university and seem headed for a career in management consultancy. But cinema is my passion. Should I follow my heart and do films, even if it seems risky?

– Florian Neumann, Germany

61

Dear Florian,

The answer depends on you – or more precisely on how you compare with rivals for these jobs. Choosing the best career is a little like trying to choose the shortest queue at the post office. (Perhaps you do not have queues at German post offices – try to imagine.) All the queues will tend to be equally long; if any of them were obviously quicker, people would already have joined them.

The only reason for you to choose one queue over another would be if you had a crush on the handsome post office clerk at window number two and nobody else did. If everyone else did, each of you would find it a toss-up as to whether to spend twice as long queuing for a chance to brush hands over the stamps or to get quick service from somebody less fanciable.

Now back to your career choice. All jobs, like all post office queues, are similarly attractive once you take into account working conditions, entry qualifications and pay. What you must consider is not whether you like creative work but whether you like it more than all the other aspiring film-makers who are keeping wages low and opportunities scarce.

Your choice to study management now makes consulting easier, and therefore relatively more attractive, compared with other potential careers. It's as though you chose a queue some time ago and are now near the front. Since you are considering joining the back of another queue, however, perhaps you are just obtuse enough to make film-making the ideal choice.

Yours, from the queue, The Undercover Economist

Dear Undercover Economist,

I recently won more than €100m on the lottery. I am terrified that the money will come between me and my friends or that I shall make a mess of spending it. What should I do?

– Anonymous of Limerick, Ireland

Dear Anonymous,

Don't worry about your friends. Even if things don't work out, with €100m in the bank you will not have any trouble making new ones. Still, you are right to be concerned about managing your win correctly.

If you were a rational economic agent you would instantly optimise your purchasing patterns to deal with your greatly expanded budget constraint. Evidently you are not, or you would certainly not have wasted money on a lottery ticket, which gave you a tiny chance of winning a prize that you now say you do not want.

Economic psychologists have long realised that people do violate the axioms of economic theory. The economist John List has demonstrated, however, that these mistakes typically happen in unfamiliar settings. With experience people do act rationally.

Therefore you must acquire this experience. I recommend putting your money in trust with binding rules on when you can withdraw it. The first year allow yourself fifty thousand euros; this should relieve immediate money worries and provide yourself, and these precious friends of yours, with a few treats. After this practice allow yourself a hundred thousand euros in the second year and two hundred thousand euros in the third. After eleven years you will have withdrawn all the money and you should have had plenty of time to think about how best to spend it. You will have acquired newer, richer friends and you may even have kept some of your old ones.

But before you become too expert with your money, kindly note that my commission on this advice is a modest 1 per cent.

Yours selflessly, The Undercover Economist

Dear Undercover Economist,

I'm a very wealthy man. It occurs to me that I might use my fortune to express my values by investing in an ethical fund. Should I?

– Anonymous, New York

Dear Anonymous,

Your actions will make no difference, even if you have billions of dollars to sling around. In principle if enough investors refuse to invest in so-called unethical companies, then such companies will face a higher cost of capital and will find it more difficult to expand their operations.

In practice this is unlikely. As long as a substantial number of investors look only at financials, they will seek out the pariah firms (oil companies, pornographers, management consultants) whenever they become cheap. The more ethical investors shun such companies, the more attractive they look to other investors.

Your decision will probably cost you, too. You often see ethical funds arguing that they achieve better performance. This is nonsense. Even if, by a staggering coincidence, the ethical companies are the only good investments, a profit-driven fund manager could pick them and do no worse than a fastidious one. The truth is, by denying yourself options your ethical investment returns will tend to be more volatile.

Some ethical funds did very well during the technology bubble because they held dotcom companies, which don't cause pollution or human rights violations. Others – such as the Ave Maria Catholic values fund – did well as the bubble deflated for the converse reason: according to financial journalist Daniel Gross it has shunned technology firms because they offer benefits to unmarried partners of employees.

Neither result proves anything about future performance. If it did you could equally consider the high-flying Vice Fund. It is invested in gambling, alcohol, defence, tobacco . . . and Microsoft.

Yours, in vice, The Undercover Economist

—————

Dear Undercover Economist,

I am experiencing the strains of being a final-year student. This semester alone I need to complete seven projects and assignments, work on my dissertation and sit five exams.

I am the captain of the karate club, which requires a big time commitment, and I am applying for graduate jobs, which means lots of interviews and assessment days in the next few months. There aren't enough hours in the day – how do I prioritise my tasks effectively?

– Derrick, via email

Dear Derrick,

Clearly you are not an economics student or you would have already solved the linear programming problem necessary to optimise your allocation of time. Let me instead give you a couple of pointers.

First, your time is spent investing rather than consuming: sitting exams and applying for jobs will expand your consumption set in the future. Under the circumstances it would be reasonable to borrow. You can borrow a little time from the future with the help of stimulants but a more practical solution is to borrow money to save time. Quit any part-time job, take taxis, hire a cleaner and order takeaways. This will save time and you can deal with the cost later when you've secured one of those precious jobs.

More fundamentally look for opportunities to gain from trade. Your karate appears to be an area of comparative advantage so perhaps you could persuade some clever weakling to write your dissertation for you. In exchange you could beat up the boyfriend of the girl he's been lusting after.

Five minutes of applied karate practice for you would be a life-transforming experience for your assistant; well worth many days of work on your dissertation. Capitalism is not always pretty.

Yours, in search of gains from trade,
The Undercover Economist

Dear Undercover Economist,

I'm hiring a cleaner to help around the house. I understand the going rate is five or six pounds an hour, but that seems low. Should I offer more?

– Harriet Trent, Highgate, London

Dear Harriet,

Classical economics says that you should not. If five pounds an hour is the market-clearing rate then that is what you need to offer. You should raise the rate only if you cannot get the vacancy filled for less.

Fancier economic theories disagree. 'Efficiency wage theory' suggests stinginess but the idea is the reverse. Advertise the job at, say, ten pounds an hour and therefore reduce turnover, increase the number of applicants and perhaps boost effort from a cleaner who knows he or she has a lot to lose from dismissal. In the long run you may do better.

Recent laboratory experiments suggest a stranger notion: advertise at five pounds an hour but then pay ten pounds. Economist psychologists argue that such an unexpected bonus will induce gratitude and extra effort.

If true, traditional economics can safely be chucked out of the window. But beware putting too much weight on laboratory work because gratitude can be short-lived.

A recent study by economists John List and Uri Gneezy shows this: they hired people to do work such as data entry or door-to-door collection for a charity, but paid some of their employees an unexpectedly high wage. As the laboratory work predicts, the grateful recipients worked extra hard. But List and Gneezy showed that the warm fuzzy feelings didn't last long – in fact until lunchtime on day one.

So if you really feel like paying twice as much, why don't you just hire two cleaners? You can feel proud of creating more employment and you should get more done too: competition is always energising.

Yours magnanimously, The Undercover Economist

Dear Undercover Economist,

To improve my chances of getting a raise should I be the first person to walk through the office door in the morning or the last person to leave at night?

– D. Clark, Seattle

Dear D. Clark,

Being first into the office is a risky business. What if you get in at 6.30 a.m. but someone else was there at 6.15 a.m.? In the winner-takes-all world you envisage, you might just as well have crawled in at 10 a.m., because there are no prizes for coming second.

Being last out of the office is at least predictable. You just wait until everyone else has gone, and barely a second longer. However, your colleagues will realise this so the last-out strategy may become popular and thus expensive. Which is the easiest path to a raise?

Strange as it may seem, both competitions are a form of auction – in both cases the bids are effort not cash, and in both cases it's not just the winner who has to pay. Nobel laureate William

Vickrey has shown, surprisingly, that all such auctions raise the same expected revenue. Both the first-in and the last-out competition will be equally profitable for your boss and equally costly for you.

I have a word of advice and a word of caution. If you want to play this game, my own research suggests that the competition will become easier to win as the year draws on and your rivals use up their reserves of energy and spousal goodwill. Take it easy at first and only burn the midnight oil once your rivals are getting divorced.

But perhaps you should not play at all. This is a competition likely to be won by whomever is most optimistic about the prospects for a juicy raise. Optimists tend to be disappointed.

Yours, last in and first out, The Undercover Economist

Dear Undercover Economist,

Why do most of us iron our clothes when we are untidy in so many other ways?

– Judith Oliver, Singapore

Dear Judith,

There is an obvious difference between an immaculate shirt and an immaculate sitting room: you get to enjoy the aesthetic benefits of tidying your living space but not – unless you spend a lot of time in front of the mirror – the aesthetic benefits of your own clothes.

After all, how many of you can honestly say you haven't sailed through the day only to discover that you have spinach between your teeth and you forgot to brush your hair? The horror is apparent to everyone but you.

So why do we care more about other people's enjoyment of our tidiness than our own? It is not a matter of selflessness: we try to make a good visual impression because it will bring us wealth, status and, we hope, a bit of sex too.

But a second question arises: why are we judged on appearances? It might be intrinsically satisfying to have a well-dressed boyfriend but there is nothing fundamentally less productive about a scruffy accountant. Evidently the tie is important because employers believe it is correlated with diligence and talent.

If this is true, we would expect to see the largest premium on snappy dressing in professions where there are few other effective ways to evaluate performance. Estate agents and management consultants are sharply dressed in the absence of more convincing guides to their competence.

In professions where talent is more obvious, this facade is not needed. That is why when I look around the *Financial Times* office, neatly pressed shirts and blouses are hard to find.

Yours rumpledly, The Undercover Economist

Dear Undercover Economist,

I enjoy my job but I think it is time to move on and have been exploring new opportunities. I have been offered a job with a rival company and I think it would be perfect but it is only a six-month position as maternity cover. If I want it, I need to say so immediately.

I might also land a job at the overseas head office of my current employer. That would suit me just as well but there will be no decisions made for several weeks. What should I do?

– Name and address supplied

Dear Anonymous,

I fear you are tangling yourself up in knots through what behavioural economists call 'hyperbolic discounting', a common but irrational obsession with having things now.

Many people would rather have ten pounds today than eleven pounds tomorrow, but ask them if they would rather have ten pounds on 30 September next year or eleven pounds the day after that, they will sensibly choose the eleven pounds a day later. Come next year, of course, they will have a change of heart.

Securing the new, cool job permanently at either company is uncertain. But if you stay with your current employer and fail to win the new job you still have your old, enjoyable job and can try again. Quit to take the job as maternity cover and if things don't work out you'll be unemployed. Taking the maternity cover looks unwise to me, but to you it simply looks immediate.

To make a more rational decision, try a thought experiment. Imagine that neither job will be available for a year, but you need to decide now, in advance, which one you will go for. The thought experiment may outwit your hyperbolic discount rate, as well as your urge to gamble your career away.

Yours hyperbolically, The Undercover Economist

Dear Undercover Economist,

After recent lay-offs a colleague and friend of mine was asked to take on some very occasional receptionist duties in addition to her regular role. My colleague has adamantly refused as she sees this as a downgrading of her skills, which she has tried very hard to build to more value-added activities. She fears that taking on the duties would hurt her 'brand equity' within the company. She is willing to quit or be fired if the company insists.

I have suggested that she pay some other colleague to do the task. My theory is that someone would be willing to do it for extra money and that my friend would be better off paying a hundred dollars per month not to do the task than losing her job over her refusal to perform the duty. Have I given my friend bum advice?

— Gigi Brienza, New Jersey

Dear Gigi,

There is nothing wrong with your idea. If more corporate employees bribed each other to do work, office life would likely be much more efficient. In fact some people might be happy to hang around the office for no salary at all in the hope of picking up some odd jobs.

But while your idea is good, your friend's strategy is brilliant.

All employers know that phrases such as 'brand equity' are all too easy to spout and that they should look instead for signs of genius in costly signals, for example, a useless but difficult degree – such as an MBA. Your friend's foot-stamping is the perfect signal of quality because it is so high-risk. In effect she is saying she is so confident of finding a new job that she refuses the tiniest imposition on her. She is likely to get her way. She sounds insufferable.

Yours, in a tantrum, The Undercover Economist

Dear Undercover Economist,

I have a big problem with my school. In Italian schools the study of Latin is required, with priority given even over studying English. The reasons given: it is the language of our ancestors and it helps us to improve our logical capacities.

I find that this is useless because we could study Chinese, which would improve our logical capacity and also help us to achieve something in the future. What do you think?

– Andrea Rocchetto (age fifteen), Rome

Dear Andrea,

It does seem puzzling. Knowing Latin appears to convey no practical benefit. Even in the politest society it is less a display of erudition, more a demonstration of a misspent youth, like being able to recite too many Monty Python sketches.

You correctly observe that Chinese would serve just as well as mental exercise and conveys the additional advantage of being able to talk to people other than the Pope. The technical term for this is that learning Latin is a 'weakly dominated' strategy: it is never superior to learning Chinese, and sometimes inferior.

Unfortunately you are up against politics here. Public-choice theory suggests that a small group with much to gain from a policy will tend to prevail against a large group who stand each to lose a small amount. The small group knows the stakes and is better organised – which is why we have trade tariffs, which help a small number of people while imposing poorly understood costs on a diffuse majority.

In your case the scattered victims are millions of suffering students, while the victors are likely to be a well-established lobby of Latin teachers. Simply ask yourself, *cui bono*? Or as they say in China, *dui shei you hao chu*?

Bene vale, The Undercover Economist

Dear Undercover Economist,

My diary is back-to-back meetings from 9 a.m. to 6 p.m. almost every day. These are not meetings I can avoid, and often I am double- and triple-booked. As well as this I have real work to do. Having delegated everything I can to my team, I still find it difficult to leave the office before 8 p.m. most days. This has gone on long enough! What should I do to get back control of my diary?

– P.M., via email

Dear P.M.,

Your diary displays communist tendencies. Your delight in Stak-hanovite posing shows the old communist confusion between input and output. This reached an extreme in Mao's great leap forward, where kitchen utensils were melted down in order to produce . . . more kitchen utensils.

You are also making the classic central-planner's error, trying to run a team without giving anybody else real decision-making authority. You say you are delegating all you can but are evidently not doing it. And with you booked to attend more meetings than there are hours in the day, I am willing to bet your subordinates know a lot more about what needs to be done than you do.

You simply need to introduce the price system into your little politburo. Charge by the hour, as do lawyers or psychiatrists. Better, auction off spaces in your diary to the highest bidder. The bidders could include clients, superiors or subordinates. If they want your attention, they'll have to find the cash.

If the total sum raised exceeds your salary, many congratula-tions! You will have justified your existence and at the same time cut out all those time-wasting, low-value activities. However, I fear that you may find less demand for your unique talents than you anticipate. Stand ready to offer a discount.

Yours, with ample time, The Undercover Economist

———————

Dear Undercover Economist,

I am a senior political figure who has just left office. I always believed that I could make up for years of badly paid public service by advising a major company for a fat retainer. I know nothing about business yet my network of contacts would be invaluable.

But somebody has just shown me a thing called 'Facebook', which they say is being used by lots of new graduates. I have been told that the economic value of my 'network' is not what it was. What is going on?

– T.B.

Dear T.B.,

Perhaps you were busy contemplating international affairs when the dotcom bubble burst?

You seem to be thinking of a simplistic model of networks in which size is everything. One fax machine can do nothing, two can talk to each other, and because each new machine can connect to the entire network, each new machine adds more value than the last. Ditto for mobile phones, eBay and Facebook: twice as big is much more than twice as valuable. Venture capitalists therefore pay big bucks for large networks, no matter how shallow.

Yet this simple arithmetic ignores an offsetting effect: diminishing marginal returns. The first mobile phones were used to conduct multi-million-dollar deals. One more mobile phone today is one more source of classroom text messages. Many people who sign up to Facebook quickly find they have no use for it.

So do not despair that your network is smaller than your son's list of Facebook friends. He may share the latest U2 single but you have Bono's phone number. There should be no trouble monetising that sort of access. Don't fritter away your retirement leisure on Facebook.

Your 'Friend', The Undercover Economist

Dear Undercover Economist,

I am an economics student and intend to run for president of the student union this year. The elections are won on the basis of whose name is seen the most around campus. Given that it is improbable I will win, I am willing to offer a pot of hundreds of pounds to people to help campaign – dependent on my winning. What is the most efficient use of this pot? Hire one person to go flat out? Or spread the money around?

– J., England

Dear J.,

If you are able to fool your potential recruits into taking you seriously, you will find willing volunteers – and you may indeed win. But you seem like an obvious loser to me. If your fellow students are as dismissive of your chances as you yourself are, they will find your offer unattractive.

They will refuse to help and you will lose. Either way your

77

situation – like that of many politicians – is dependent on a self-fulfilling prophecy.

You need to find some way to take advantage of your position as a hopeless outsider. I would recommend putting a decent bet on yourself to win – you should be able to find long odds. The prospective winnings would make your offer more generous, which could make all the difference.

As for how to divide the money, I recommend that you run a prize draw, winning volunteer takes all. That would make the cash payment more attractive when your campaign is sparsely supported and the incentive is most needed.

In any case the economist John List has shown that prize draws are a great way to raise money for charity. Your campaign certainly sounds like a charity case to me.

Yours charitably, The Undercover Economist

Dear Undercover Economist,

My boss swears that compensation in our corporation is based upon pay-for-performance. Is that an economic reality?

– Bob, Texas

Dear Bob,

It is certainly possible to pay people for performance and get good results for your trouble. In one case that has become famous among economists, a company that replaced cracked windscreens switched from paying workers by the hour to paying workers by the windscreen, with a penalty for repairs that later failed. Slow workers quit, fast workers worked yet faster, and faulty installations fell.

Such stories fuel the appetite for performance pay but for most jobs it is not so easy to quantify performance. Even if managers know who is doing a good job, managerial impressions cannot be written into contracts. Worse, many performance contracts expose staff to financial risks that have nothing to do with their performance. It is hardly motivational to blame your ice-cream division for missing targets during a wet summer.

So performance pay is often awarded in relative terms, such as a promotion for the top three sales staff rather than a bonus per sale. Such schemes are often called workplace tournaments because there are winners and losers.

Workplace tournaments seem to work well – perhaps a bit too well. In one study of manufacturing companies, tournament pay motivated workers to take less sick leave. It also motivated workers to refuse to lend equipment to their colleagues. After all, you can win by making colleagues look bad.

If your workplace is full of uncooperative colleagues who stab you in the back, then congratulations: your corporation does indeed pay for performance.

Yours cooperatively, The Undercover Economist

Dear Undercover Economist,

My economics tutor says that I should be studying harder if I want to do well in my exams. I think that he is basing his advice on purely theoretical assumptions and that there is no empirical evidence for his assertion. Who is right?

– M.W., Cambridge

Dear M.W.,

You're probably correct that his advice is not based on empirical research – not because no research exists but because it is very recent. But I am sorry to report that his wild speculations have now been confirmed by an intriguing natural experiment.

Previous researchers have struggled to establish a causal link between exam results and time spent studying. That is not a surprise. Bright students might work harder because they enjoy the work. Or failing students might cram to rescue their grades. Untangling the statistics seems impossible.

Yet the puzzle has been resolved by Todd Stinebrickner, an economist, and his father, mathematician Ralph Stinebrickner. Equipped with detailed time-use questionnaires, they looked at students who were randomly assigned a room-mate with a games console. Neither the students nor their room-mates differed in, say, initial test score, time spent boozing or sleeping. But students whose room-mates had video games spent less time studying and more playing Final Fantasy XII. Pure chance – the assignment of a room-mate – seems to affect time spent studying and no other important decisions. And yes, the grades did suffer.

If the analysis is correct, an extra hour a day studying has a very substantial impact on test scores – enough to lift a typical student into the top third. Unless you know some very good computer games, that is likely to be a rational investment of your time.

Yours studiously, The Undercover Economist

———————

Dear Undercover Economist,

I am in doubt whether it is worth changing school for my last year of A-Levels. I would be living in a much better place (Cambridge, whereas I am now in Dover) and getting more tuition. I am likely to have better accommodation, more freedom and will meet people with diverse interests. But is it worth the risk of not getting into university or getting lower grades on my A-Levels?

Please help me to solve this dilemma.

– G.P., Dover

Dear G.P.,

Let us run through this supposed dilemma again. You are considering a move to a place that appears to be better in every dimension, including the academic one. Yet you are hesitant because of a perceived risk.

I am tempted to recommend you consult a shrink rather than an economist. Fortunately so-called behavioural economists combine the best qualities of economist and psychologist. And any behavioural economist would quickly diagnose that you are a victim of the 'endowment effect'.

The endowment effect is an irrational preference to keep what you have rather than switch. Better the devil you know and all that.

A typical experiment designed to reveal the effect would give participants a small gift for participating in the experiment. Later the participants would be invited to swap the gift for an alternative. No matter what the original gift was, or what the alternative is, people, irrationally, are reluctant to make the swap.

Your attachment to substandard lodgings and scant tuition in Dover is clearly irrational. Move to Cambridge at once. You may be wrong, of course, but a risk of error is no excuse for inaction.

Yours decisively, The Undercover Economist

Dear Undercover Economist,

My girlfriend and I were planning to fly to Frankfurt on a budget airline. We were offered travel insurance, which I didn't think was worth the £4.95. Still, my girlfriend insisted on both of us taking the insurance. Assuming the chance of surviving a plane crash is negligible, you do not get to enjoy the benefits of the insurance should a disaster happen. Most likely your family will get paid for your death. So the worst-case scenario is that you're £4.95 poorer and dead; or at best alive, but still £4.95 poorer. What is the rationality of taking out the insurance?

– Farid Daim, Nottingham

Dear Farid,

I sympathise with your reluctance to pay for insurance but I do not follow your reasoning. There is nothing irrational about life insurance per se (although it is an unattractive product to someone with no dependants – or a selfish disposition). Overall, though, life insurance is one of very few types of insurance it is rational to purchase because it protects against the risk of a dramatic loss. Another is insurance against catastrophic medical expenses, another role for travel insurance; but you may not be bothered about this, as EU citizens get cheap healthcare in member countries.

So it seems to me that you purchased 'rucksack insurance'. Petty insurance is highly profitable – which is why it is bundled with cheap flights. But it is unnecessary. Over the course of your life you will earn thousands of times the price of your rucksack and contents. It is better to save on premiums and take occasional losses on the chin – you'll come out well ahead in the long run. I have.

Take heart, though. You saw the bigger picture and did exactly what your girlfriend told you. Smart move.

Safe travels, The Undercover Economist

Dear Undercover Economist,

I am amazed by people who stand outside in front of the opening doors of trains and lifts knowing full well that the people inside will have to exit before they can enter. Obstructing the exiters will only delay them, and the enterers seem to be in such a rush that this is surely not in their best interests. What is astonishing is that this is a universal phenomenon. Explain!

– Nazir Kazi

Dear Nazir,

I too have observed this phenomenon with trains but more rarely with lifts, and I think that suggests an explanation.

It is true that by obstructing people who are leaving the train, people may delay it by a few seconds.

A few seconds' delay to everyone on the train is an appreciable social loss but scarcely matters to the selfish individual in question.

True, a delay is a delay.

But you have misinterpreted what such people are aiming to do. They are not trying to hasten the departure of the train; they are trying to get a seat. That means being the first into the carriage just as seats are being vacated, which in turn means standing in front of the opening doors and generally getting in everybody's way.

It is a classic prisoner's dilemma: everyone would be better off if everyone hung back, but each individual does better for himself by pushing forward.

It is not surprising that this behaviour is more unusual when it comes to lifts. Lifts do not have seats and usually have room to accommodate everyone who is waiting.

The behaviour you describe is selfish, but it is not irrational.

Yours courteously, The Undercover Economist

Dear Undercover Economist,

The law of comparative advantage suggests people should use their talent but we're also told 'do what you love'. What if I have no talent for what I love? Is it worth time and effort pursuing a dream career I'm no good at?

– Joy

Dear Joy,

Your letter is intelligent but it is also opaque: you do not reveal what your dream career is. Still, a lack of facts has never been an obstacle to economic analysis so this is no time for methodological scruples. The principle of comparative advantage states that you should focus on what you do best, relative to the standard set by everybody else. You can do accounts and use the money to hire a cook or do cooking and use the money to hire an accountant; the correct choice depends not just on whether you are a good bean-sheller and a poor bean-counter but on whether the world is full of better cooks and worse accountants.

There is no conflict between this principle and the idea that you should 'do what you love'. Being good at a job means you will earn more; enjoying a job means you will not mind earning less. Decide whether you prefer money or fun.

But what if you are incapable of doing any job you enjoy? Well, your career is not the be all and end all. Economist Andrew Oswald believes we work too hard and under-invest in friendships. So if my career advice is depressing, ignore it and talk to your friends instead.

Yours comparatively, The Undercover Economist

Dear Undercover Economist,

I have been invited to give a presentation at a conference. Naturally I'd like to look as good as possible. I have been given some flexibility over length, topic, timing and so on. What advice can you give me and is it best for me to open or close the proceedings?

– Jeremy L., London

Dear Jeremy,

Anyone can tell you the obvious stuff: don't use boring bullet-point slides and keep it simple. Obvious, but most people, at the expense of their audience, ignore this advice.

Let me instead focus on a less-obvious insight, discovered by the economist Lionel Page and his wife, the psychologist Katie Page. The Pages looked at years of results from talent contests such as *X-Factor* and *American Idol*, in which contestants perform and viewers vote as to who they'd like to see again.

The Pages were able to measure whether it was an advantage to appear first or last, or immediately after a flop or a show-stopper. Because most singers appeared several times, the Pages could take account of the fact that the show's producers might deliberately open and close with strong performers. In effect they looked at what happened to the same contestant when they appeared earlier or later.

The bottom line is that it's OK to go first but better to go last. A partial explanation is that these acts are easier to remember. Obscurity doesn't seem to attract you so make sure you're closing the show.

Yours show-stoppingly, The Undercover Economist

Dear Undercover Economist,

My employer has just instituted a new mentoring scheme and as a relatively new recruit I'm eligible. I can't make up my mind whether this is an important opportunity to learn or a colossal waste of everybody's time.

Any thoughts?

– Ben Harmison

Dear Ben,

Some new research by Jonah Rockoff, an economist at Columbia University, is possibly of interest to you. Rockoff studied an acclaimed mentoring programme for New York City teachers. He adjusted for confounding factors – such as the fact that duff teachers may get more mentoring help, making it seem that mentors reduce teaching standards.

Rockoff found some evidence that the programme encouraged teachers to stay in their jobs and improved the achievements of their students. If his results apply more widely, they suggest that the thing you are most likely to learn from a mentor is how to operate in your particular company, rather than picking up transferable skills.

But the effects seem rather modest. Why, then, is mentoring so popular? Rockoff finds that teachers are convinced that their mentors have helped their teaching skills even if the effect is not obvious from their students' results. Overall I'd suggest that you go for this mentoring scheme. It will make you look cooperative and you might even learn something – but even if it is useless you'll still convince yourself it was time well spent.

Your mentor, The Undercover Economist

Dear Undercover Economist,

The offer of a new job means I have the chance to move from sunny Assisi, the home of Saint Francis, to Luxembourg, one of the rainiest and cloudiest places in Europe. Of course the move will mean I have a better salary but how much value should I place on the weather?

– Simone

Dear Simone,

Lacking a hedonimeter, I cannot tell how much you love the sunshine. But I can tell you what others in your position have done.

Superficially it seems that many people seek sunny climes, especially now that air conditioning is available. For example, long-run population growth in the 'Sunbelt' – the US South – is often attributed to a demand for, well, sun.

Harvard economists Ed Glaeser and Kristina Tobio think otherwise. They argue that before 1980 the boom in the South was thanks to the region's growing productivity. After 1980 population continued to grow but house prices lagged behind those elsewhere in the US, suggesting that the driving force was not high demand but permissive planning rules. Certainly balmy California, with its tighter restrictions on building, did not enjoy the same population growth.

All of this tends to suggest that people don't value sunshine quite as much as is supposed. In other words don't expect too much compensation for moving to Luxembourg: your more weatherproof rivals will do the job for less.

Yours, from sunny climes, The Undercover Economist

Dear Undercover Economist,

I am about to leave university and have received employment offers from management consulting firms in both London and New York. I have to say that I like the idea of living in either one of these global cities – the question is which one should I plump for?

R.A., Cambridge, UK

Dear R.A.,

Congratulations on asking the right question. Too many people relocate based on a nice job offer – or love affair – without considering the significance of the geographical decision. The economist and urbanophile Richard Florida argues that your choice of city is the most important decision you can make because it determines job options, the quality of your everyday life, your love life and much else.

That said, you seem to have made this decision already. Cities such as Seattle, Berlin, Dar es Salaam, Hong Kong and Moscow each offer something unique, but it is hard to see much difference between New York and London. In fact London has more in common with New York than any British city.

If you must restrict your choice, you are at least taking advantage of the trend for the big global cities to become ever more dominant. Perhaps you should consider New York: you have a network of friends in the UK; New York would diversify your life experiences and expand your networks. And apparently if you can make it there, you can make it anywhere.

Yours urbanely, The Undercover Economist

Efficient Protocols for the Lavatory Seat
Family Life

An old saying puts it this way: you can choose your friends but you can't choose your relatives. Like many old sayings, it is not quite true. Prospective parents temporarily assume a near godlike responsibility: to decide how many human lives to create and when to try to create them. As we shall see, this important decision can be illuminated by thinking of children as consumer durables.

Sadly this analogy does not continue to be helpful once you actually have children, and 'Dear Economist' is swamped with letters asking for advice on how to get the little blighters to behave. Fortunately, from applications of game theory to the 'rotten kid theorem' of a Nobel Prize winner, economics has much to say about sharing a household with small utility-maximisers – and, when they're grown up and you're approaching your dotage, about how to get them to visit you more often.

The other big family decisions revolve around our spouses. Here we move beyond dating questions to address problems about the toils and the spoils of a mature relationship: who should look after the children, who gets the house after the divorce and, most critically, who should take responsibility for the angle of elevation of the lavatory seat? Economics has a well-developed literature on negotiations and on dividing up costs and benefits. These letters test that literature to its limits.

Dear Undercover Economist,

My husband and I have two bonny children already and
another on the way. But the eldest child, Alasdair, is
becoming wilful and we have a problem with discipline.
We threaten punishment but he misbehaves anyway and
then we don't have the heart to punish him. Is there
anything you can suggest?

– Sylvia Graham, Edinburgh

Dear Sylvia,

Let's think about the problem logically. Game theory is the tool
of choice for any such interaction. First, Alasdair decides whether
to be naughty. Then you decide whether or not to punish him.
He prefers to be naughty only if unpunished and you prefer only
to threaten punishments that are not carried out.

There are two equilibria to the game: the one you complain
about, when he is naughty and you do not punish him; and the
one you want, when you punish him if he is naughty but don't
have to carry out the punishment because he is good.

If the second equilibrium sounds implausible, that's because it
is. Economists call this a 'non-subgame-perfect equilibrium': in
other words when Alasdair calls your bluff you back down.

No wonder you find yourself in the unwanted, subgame-perfect
equilibrium. Economists have long known that in a one-off situation you will never make your threat credible. But never fear, you
will play this game again and again, both with Alasdair and your
younger children. That changes the dynamic completely.

It is crucial to establish a reputation for toughness. Remember that when you punish Alasdair, you have lost the battle but are winning the war: the discomfort of imposing discipline should be weighed against the future misbehaviour you are preventing. As your reputation as a disciplinarian becomes established, your children's behaviour will improve.

Perhaps this all seems like common sense but you should be aware that two Nobel Prizes have been awarded for this analysis. Economists have worked hard to demonstrate to you that sometimes you have to be cruel to be kind.

Yours subgame perfectly, The Undercover Economist

Dear Undercover Economist,

I am secretary of a local baby-sitting circle and I have a problem. Members are simply not going out enough – everybody is trying to build up a reserve of baby-sitting coupons. But if nobody goes out, nobody baby-sits and nobody builds the reserve they desire. Should we introduce rules compelling people to go out, say, twice a month?

– Mrs Janine Broughton, Lowestoft

Dear Mrs Broughton,

Your baby-sitting circle is in recession.

This is hardly surprising: you are running tight monetary

policy, have constitutionally rigid prices, and suffer severe capital market failures.

You are correct in thinking that as long as everybody is trying to save simultaneously they will all be frustrated and the circle will never work well. Forcing people to go out and hire baby-sitters will create the illusion of economic activity but there is no guarantee that your centrally planned solution will be what people really wanted.

A simple fix would be to create a spot of inflation. This worked well for Mr and Mrs R.J. Sweeney, as described in their famous paper 'Monetary Theory and the Great Capitol Hill Baby-Sitting Co-op Crisis'. If everybody is issued with extra baby-sitting coupons, they will all feel that they have the reserve they need and start hiring each other more freely. The risk is that inflation gets out of hand and too many baby-sitting coupons start chasing too few willing baby-sitters.

An alternative would be to set up a coupon bank that lends coupons out at an agreed rate of interest. If too few people are willing to go out, lower the rate of interest; if there are too many baby-sitters, raise it.

You may wish to establish some kind of committee to decide interest rates.

The value of coupons should also be allowed to float. In winter, when few people wish to go out and everybody is glad enough of a warm evening watching television with other people's children, the value of coupons will rise.

Come the summer, coupons will not buy much baby-sitting. This price flexibility will work better than the most ingenious central banker.

Yours stimulatively, The Undercover Economist

———————

Dear Undercover Economist,

My son has just passed his driving test but he drives like a lunatic.

I am sure it's only a matter of time before he has an accident but now he has his eyes on a clapped-out second-hand car that I'm sure won't provide him with much protection. I've even been considering buying him something a bit more sturdy just to improve his chances. Do you think this is a good idea?

– Tricia Stott, Wilmslow

Dear Ms Stott,

You are proposing an engineering solution to a psychological problem. You say your son drives like a lunatic but it may be more helpful to think of him as preferring speed and fun to safety. Given these preferences his driving style is rational.

It may not help if you put him in a safer car. But if his car was equipped with nitro-glycerine in the boot and spikes on the steering column your son might be encouraged to drive more carefully.

On the other hand a car with many safety features lowers the danger of exciting driving and your son would rationally choose more excitement. This phenomenon is called the 'Peltzman Effect', after economist Sam Peltzman, who found that safer cars led to more casual driving, more accidents, roughly the same number of driver deaths and an increase in pedestrian casualties. Although the Peltzman Effect remains controversial, some subsequent research has reached similar conclusions. Peltzman's work suggests that if your son is confident in his car's safety features, his swashbuckling driving style will compensate for them.

The solution is obvious: make sure your son believes his car is dangerous. Let him buy his second-hand car but insist that it goes for a service. Get the mechanics to secretly install air-bags and anti-lock brakes, all the while shaking their heads about what a 'beast' the car is.

Yours duplicitously, The Undercover Economist

Dear Undercover Economist,

We have been happily married for over fifty years but there is a fly in the ointment. Our three adult children stand to inherit a sizeable sum when we pass away but we hardly feel they deserve it. They rarely call and never visit. What do you suggest?

– Mr and Mrs Lear, Sunderland

Dear Mr and Mrs Lear,

I am sorry to hear about the neglectful behaviour of your children. Love cannot be compelled, not even by the most skilled economist, but that need not be a problem. You appear to be more concerned about the behaviour of your children than about whether they truly love you, and while their love cannot be compelled, their attention can.

The obvious solution is to threaten to disinherit any child who does not meet your quota of (for example) two phone calls a week and four visits a year.

The trouble is that your children may realise that, as loving parents, you are unwilling to disinherit all three of them and send the money to the Battersea Dogs and Cats Home. As long as they are talking to each other they will outsmart such a crass bluff.

Fortunately the solution to this problem has been produced by economists Avinash Dixit and Barry Nalebuff. The trick is to destabilise the equilibrium in which your children neglect you by informing them that, while you will give equal shares to anyone who meets the quota, if all children fail to meet the quota you will give the full bequest to the one who makes the largest number of phone calls. When your children realise that even a single phone call might make the difference between receiving everything and receiving nothing, there will be no stable equilibrium short of everybody paying you the attention you crave.

Yours, in equilibrium, The Undercover Economist

Dear Undercover Economist,

My husband and I are not believers but we think it might be a good idea to give our children some kind of religious upbringing. What would you suggest?

– Mrs Rachel Harris, York

Dear Mrs Harris,

This question must weigh on the minds of many parents since it seems that religious belief has profound financial implications. Consider church attendance, for example: time spent going to church is time that cannot be devoted either to leisure or to work. This seems to be a serious cost but it might have hidden benefits: your children could make important business contacts at church and gain access to an informal social security network.

Religion is also about faith. If you teach your children a strict code of ethics, enforced by belief in heaven and hell, they may behave with more integrity. Does this mean they will be exploited or will they earn more trust?

Obviously pure theory can only get you so far on this question but economists such as Robert Barro and Rachel McCleary have put in the statistical legwork. It turns out that believing in God has no appreciable economic effect but a belief in heaven and hell is just the carrot and stick to boost economic growth. The results on church attendance cut the other way: whatever networking your children will do at church, it seems that the time would be more profitably spent pressing the flesh elsewhere.

Your problem, therefore, is to find a religion with a firm line on right and wrong but a minimal time commitment. Take comfort from the fact that countries with religious competition, like Britain, produce more efficient religions, with stronger beliefs for a given time spent in church. All you need to do now is shop around.

Yours devoutly, The Undercover Economist

Dear Undercover Economist,

I'm afraid to say that my wife and I are getting divorced. We are struggling to work out how to divide our possessions, especially the house. Our arguments are only making a bad situation worse. Is there a solution?

– Mr B. Graham, Kent

Dear Mr Graham,

You have my sympathy. Because so many of these shared items have sentimental value, it is hard to come to an amicable agreement. Bluntly speaking, you are both lying about your true preferences to manipulate the bargaining process and get more of the stuff you want.

Economists were for a while pessimistic about solving such problems as the incentive to lie typically makes it impossible to trade an object of sentimental value efficiently. The buyer wants to downplay the value and the seller wants to exaggerate it, and the trade is scuppered.

But game theorists Robert Gibbons, Peter Cramton and Paul Klemperer have demonstrated that when an object is jointly owned and one partner must buy out the other an efficient outcome is easy enough to reach.

Professor Klemperer says that you and your wife must each write down an offer for half the house.

If you name the higher price, you get the house and must pay your wife for her half of it. The price you pay is the average of the prices you each wrote down.

You will be far less tempted to lie because if you bid too low you have to sell the house cheaply. However, if you bid too high you pay dearly for it. You can follow the same process for every object if you wish.

I have only one word of caution. As Professor Klemperer is happily married to his first wife, his advice is presumably straight from the ivory tower.

Yours efficiently, The Undercover Economist

Dear Undercover Economist,

My wedding anniversary is fast approaching. What should I get my wife to show her how much I love her?

– Malcolm Hayfield, Whitstable

Dear Mr Hayfield,

That depends on how much you love her. If you think she would be pleased to know, best to make a clear signal of your ardour. If the grubby truth is that love's flame burns less brightly than once it did, better to hide in the mainstream of mediocrity.

Good examples of also-ran gifts are flowers and chocolates – always appreciated, not too expensive. Your wife will be unable to tell whether she is unloved or you are merely uninspired.

Your question suggests, however, that you conceive of your love as something to shout about from the rooftops. The simple solution, then, is to buy something hugely expensive as a signal that you expect many more years of wedded bliss. A less ardent husband, who expected fewer years or less bliss, would never choose to give such a signal.

Your choices do not end there. Any expensive signal will serve – even burning fifty-pound notes in front of her. But not all signals convey equivalent overtones. Buying risqué underwear does not convey the same message as giving your wife stock in Vodafone, even if the price tag is identical.

Your final consideration should therefore be to give a present that nobody would think of if they did not completely understand your wife's dreams and desires. Whether it is a specially commissioned oil painting of her favourite place, or the signed Stone Roses memorabilia that recalls her wild youth, this is your triumph. Your gift will signal first that you remembered the anniversary, second that you are committed to the marriage and, finally, that you understand the wife.

Yours romantically, The Undercover Economist

Dear Undercover Economist,

How do I stop my ten-year-old daughter thumping her little brother?

– Cynthia Evans, Richmond, Yorkshire

Dear Cynthia,

I am puzzled by your problem. Nobel laureate Gary Becker proved, in his celebrated 'rotten kid theorem', that such thumping should occur only when socially efficient. A numerical example may help here. Assume that you care equally about yourself and your children, and so spread a weekly budget of £750 worth of love, attention and money equally between the three of you.

Converting pleasure and pain into monetary terms, if your daughter were to punch her brother, he would suffer, say, £20 worth of hurt, and she would gain £5 of sadistic pleasure. This would reduce your family budget by £15. Your optimal response would be to spread the loss, equalising post-thump incomes. He would get £265 (minus £20 of thump), she would get £240 (plus £5 of thump) and you £245. Your daughter ends up worse off and can be expected to restrain her urges.

Of course it is possible that your daughter enjoys attacking her brother more than he dislikes it. If she gains £20 worth of pleasure and he loses £5, she has generated a surplus of £15 which your redistribution will spread equally among the three of you. This would make her attacks both individually rational and socially optimal.

If your daughter is still assaulting her brother after your redistributive efforts, it demonstrates that she is enjoying it. There are three possibilities: your daughter is irrational; your son doesn't much mind getting thumped; or you are simply failing to do the maths.

Yours rottenly, The Undercover Economist

My sixteen-year-old son has been in trouble with the police for graffiti and other offences. Despite getting very good GCSEs he has now left school, has no job and seems bent on ruining his prospects and his family life. How can I get him to realise that his expenditure must be less than his income and that he is responsible for getting an income?

– Elaine Spooncer, Manchester

Dear Elaine,

You wish your son to stay within the law, rejoin the educational system, get some kind of job and then spend less than he earns? Presumably then you can stop for breakfast before ticking further things off your 'to do' list.

History is littered with governments which failed to appreciate that you cannot achieve two policy objectives with one policy instrument. For example we might expect Mervyn King at the Bank of England to prevent deflation, pop house-price bubbles, or temporarily push the economy towards full employment. Since he controls only one instrument, interest rates, we would be foolish to demand all three at once.

Your three objectives require three separate policy instruments. Preventing criminal behaviour requires a firm hand – perhaps delegation to an independent regulator (your local bobby) may be necessary. Your son may then be persuaded to take A-levels if offered a credible financial incentive on completion.

But persuading him to live within his means may prove more difficult. In principle there is no problem: cut him off and let him provide for himself. Credit card companies will not oblige him for long and he will soon learn the meaning of 'budget constraint'. But you need to convince him that you do not care if he starves. The fact that you are writing to me for advice suggests otherwise.

Yours instrumentally, The Undercover Economist

Dear Undercover Economist,

My fiancé and I are trying for a baby. Should we be praying for a boy or a girl?

– Felicia Young, Bangor

Dear Felicia,

Since you are affianced I presume that you are hoping to enjoy a marriage along with your new baby. If so you will be intrigued to hear that if you become pregnant with a boy, you're more likely to be married by the time you give birth.

This is just one of a number of fascinating conclusions reached by economists Gordon Dahl and Enrico Moretti, based on a sample of three million people. Others include the fact that couples with no male children are more likely to divorce than those with only boys and that such couples are also more likely to have further children – perhaps trying for the elusive male scion. Divorced mothers with no sons are less likely to remarry and those who do remarry are more likely to divorce again.

The intuitive conclusion is that most fathers don't bother to stick around for daughters. As the proud father of a young daughter myself, I'd like to offer an alternative explanation, from Dahl's colleague Steven Landsburg.

Evolutionary biologists tell us that wealth and status are more important for the success (especially reproductive success) of boys relative to girls. Most women can have a few babies but men are capable of producing dozens, or none at all, depending on their luck and status. This suggests that parents of boys would go to some lengths to avoid a wealth-destroying divorce, while the prospects of girls are more resilient.

My conclusion is that if your marriage works out well, any child will be a blessing. If you have a boy and your marriage turns sour, you'll be forced to tough it out. Pray for the girl.

Yours sexistly, The Undercover Economist

Dear Undercover Economist,

Two years ago my wife and I divorced on fairly amicable terms and I now live alone (with the cat) in our former home. The problem is my ex-wife is still present in that her stamp is still on the house – decor, furniture, etc. I get hopelessly emotional if I want to change anything and I simply don't have her talent for making a home. How can I move on?

– Mr B., West Country

Dear Mr B.,

You should have no trouble hiring a designer or securing advice from friends. Your problem lies elsewhere. Essentially you are trapped in a situation of time inconsistency: you write suggesting that you would like to rid yourself of the furniture your ex-wife chose but admit that you don't have the spine to go through with it.

Governments suffer similarly. They promise low tax rates to encourage businesses to invest but nobody believes they will be able to stick to the promise, so they get the worst of both worlds: low taxes and low investment. If some binding commitment could be made, everyone would be better off. The clever leader writers of the *FT* recently compared such commitments to Odysseus's idea of tying himself to his ship's mast to listen to the siren song in safety.

You too could commit yourself by going on holiday and instructing a trusted friend to sell the contents of the house while you are away. But I have my qualms about helping one side of your split personality. Sometimes you wish to wipe the slate clean; at other times you want to preserve your memories. What business has an economist choosing one of these emotions over another?

Perhaps you just need to forget your obsession with interior design. Your inspiration should come from Alexander, not Odysseus. Cut through the Gordian knot: get out and find yourself a girlfriend.

Yours bluntly, The Undercover Economist

Dear Undercover Economist,

I am starting to suspect that my husband is having an affair – how can I find out?

– Mrs F., Oxford

Dear Mrs F.,

I recommend that you use an 'information market'. These markets pay out if certain events occur; for example if a certain politician was to win an election. They have an excellent record, outperforming opinion polls when it comes to forecasting election results. Such markets work well because they allow different people, each of whom may hold some important piece of information, to register their view anonymously. Confident forecasters can make their views carry extra weight by betting more.

Companies such as Hewlett Packard have operated internal information markets to make sales and production forecasts – they work better than the bureaucratic method because they uncover hidden information in a situation where people may be afraid to speak frankly. You are in a similar predicament. Whatever friends tell you, you will find it hard to know whether it is the truth. But they may be more willing to let their wallets do the talking.

Practically speaking you need to bet with people that your husband will not be proved to be having an affair by the end of 2010. Every month use eBay to auction pairs of promissory notes: one that will pay a hundred pounds if your husband is caught and one that will pay a hundred pounds if he is not. Advertise. If people are willing to offer only five pounds for the 'pay when guilty' note, the market believes your husband is blameless. If the 'pay when unproven' promise sells for a mere fiver, you can conclude that somebody – maybe everybody – believes your hubby is a love-rat.

Of course your husband may submit fake bids in an attempt to rig the market. But do not worry. Such rigging is virtually impossible in a liquid market and it will cost that slimeball dearly to try.

Your informer, The Undercover Economist

Dear Undercover Economist,

My husband and I have a son and we're thinking of having one or two more children. But how many, do you think?

– Emma Travers, York

Dear Emma,

When optimising your investment in children it's erroneous to consider quantity without thinking of quality. The most famous economist to make this mistake was Malthus: he predicted that whenever household incomes rose, families would expand to consume the new resources.

Malthus did not anticipate advances in contraception, which make it much more likely that people like you can have exactly the number of children they desire. An equally important error – if a more subtle one – was his failure to appreciate that as incomes rise parents can increase their investment in children not just by having more but by spending more time and money on each child.

In the analysis of the Nobel laureate Gary Becker, you can increase the quality of your children as well as their quantity, for example by investing in their education. Becker understood that children can be analysed in the same way as other durable consumer goods, such as cars.

Nobody would make Malthus's mistake by assuming that millionaires buy dozens of cheap cars. We all realise that a more typical response to rising income is to replace the Skoda with a Mercedes. It is hard to give you more specific advice without knowing more about your situation, but if you appreciate that your choice is between two high-quality children and three lower-quality children, things may become clearer in your mind.

Some people protest that children cannot be traded off against other consumer durables, or even analysed in the same way. Perhaps. But it's interesting to note how many of these people have few children but nice cars.

Yours procreatively, The Undercover Economist

Dear Undercover Economist,

Parents often find that some of their children turn out wealthier than others. Doting but logical parents sometimes try to even the balance by helping less successful children at the expense of the wealthier ones.

So is one better off being lazy and a failure in life in order to maximise the potential help from one's parents?

– Alexander Ross, London

Dear Mr Ross,

'Doting but logical' describes the parents of Robert Barro's macroeconomic models and Gary Becker's economic theory of the family. Such parents make sure that all children enjoy equal levels of utility, and achieve this by giving larger transfers to poorer children. Perhaps you hope that your own parents are Barro-Becker altruists. If so you could guarantee an increased handout by earning less. Slacking would seem to be, on the face of things, attractive. Think again.

If your parents truly are Barro-Becker altruists, they will ensure that the post-bequest utilities of all children are equalised: everyone will get an equal share of the total wealth generated by the parents and all siblings. By slacking, you simply reduce the size of the pie that your parents will eventually divide equally.

Your only hope would be that your parents are naive and that they will favour you, the loser, without working through the maths. What are the chances?

Most parents divide bequests equally between children, and unequal bequests are often designed to repay more devoted children. The economists Audrey Light and Kathleen McGarry analysed interviews with more than three thousand mothers with at least two adult children. Just 1 per cent said they planned to make unequal bequests because one child had greater needs than the others. Slack off if you like but you're gambling on long odds.

Yours equitably, The Undercover Economist

Dear Undercover Economist,

For cultural reasons I am probably going to have an arranged marriage, in which my parents will help choose a wife for me. This will mean that I won't have an opportunity to cohabit first to find out how well things would work. I would have to take a decision that is more rational than emotional. There are a lot of things that I would like in a woman but hardly anyone has it all. What can you advise?

– Josh Gopal, by email

Dear Josh,

When we elect members of parliament, we are the 'principals' and they are the 'agents' who, supposedly, represent us. Similarly when shareholders elect a board of directors to maximise shareholder value, the directors are their agents. Those directors will hire managers to do their bidding; again the managers are the agents.

Think for a moment: are principals ever happy with what their agents get up to? You can understand why economists speak of something called the 'principal-agent problem'.

Your parents are acting as your agents in this case. How are you to encourage them to see your point of view?

The best way forward is probably to pay them by results. Perhaps your parents should post a bond of a hundred thousand pounds, to be repaid at the rate of five thousand pounds a year plus interest as long as you and your beloved remain hitched. If you and your wife end up divorced, you keep the remaining money.

Of course your parents may be asking themselves what is in it for them. You may find that you are the one who has to post the performance bond and will get your money back only if they choose poorly. Your parents will also fret that you will connive a divorce just to lay your hands on the cash. Nobody said this was going to be easy.

Your loyal agent, The Undercover Economist

Dear Undercover Economist,

How many gifts should I register on my wedding list to optimise my total utility?

– Claire Song, via email

Dear Claire,

The wedding list reflects a rare piece of honesty in our social dealings: the admission that you do not expect your guests to choose particularly apt gifts. If only we could adopt the same candour when it comes to Christmas and birthdays the world would surely be a better place.

Nevertheless the wedding list remains fraught with potential inefficiencies and you have evidently been thinking about that. If the list is too expansive you risk guests choosing the least preferred options: you will get the frilly lavatory roll holders while the quality saucepan set will go unpurchased. (I was married not so very long ago – I feel your pain.)

On the other hand if the wedding list is too small you may find that the gifts run out and the guests decide to pick something a bit more 'original' – obviously a disaster. Equally bad, you may find that willing guests don't buy a gift at all.

The solution is a little labour-intensive but probably worth the effort. You need to release your wedding list in several tranches. Start with a selection of high-priority stuff and keep an eye on progress. When the choice is starting to wear a little thin, add the B-list gifts. If they too start to be snapped up, then unveil the C-list. Modern technology makes this fairly easy to do.

Of course this is still a hassle. For my own wedding I planned to dispense with the gift list and instead charge for admission. That seemed much simpler all round but my fiancée vetoed the idea.

I am not sure why.

Yours, in frustration, The Undercover Economist

Dear Undercover Economist,

My wife and I can't agree about how much television to let our sons (aged four and two) watch. She is more tolerant of TV, perhaps because she spends more time looking after them and needs a rest. How can we break the deadlock?

– Paul Mitchell, Wendover, Bucks

Dear Mr Mitchell,

I am not sure that you truly disagree here. You and your wife both wish your children to excel at school. Your wife wants some quiet time and your sons want to watch the box. There is only a problem if these requirements are mutually exclusive.

They do not seem to be. A new working paper by economists Matthew Gentzkow and Jesse Shapiro of Chicago University looks at the effect of television on children's test scores and future careers – and finds an effect that is small and positive. For children whose parents do not speak English the effect is stronger.

Previous studies confused the effects of television with the family circumstances that encourage children to watch it. I am willing to bet that the children of fathers with string vests also tend to do poorly at school, but the string vests are not to blame.

Gentzkow and Shapiro look at the spread of television across the US. New York had television in 1940, but Denver had to wait until 1952. Wherever television was available, children would watch for three or so hours a day – with little educational programming and plenty of commercials. So if television is bad for you, the brains of young New Yorkers should have rotted earlier than those of young Denverites. They did not.

Forget your prejudices and settle down for an educational day with Big Bird. You might learn something.

Yours, with square eyes, The Undercover Economist

Dear Undercover Economist,

Should I leave the lavatory seat down, as my wife demands? Or, with gravity on her side, should she be lowering it herself?

– Michael Govind, Cirencester

Dear Michael,

Jay Pil Choi, a (male) economist at Michigan State University, has demonstrated what men find obvious and women seem unable to grasp: that the 'status quo' rule (leave it how it was when you finished) is more efficient than the 'down' rule (put it down afterwards) under most plausible assumptions. The reasoning is that the seat should be moved only when necessary – just before someone uses the lavatory.

If a man visits the lavatory twice in a row, the 'status quo' rule saves the cost of lowering the seat when leaving only to raise it when returning. Choi also shows, using some fancy maths, that the 'status quo' rule is still superior even if the inconvenience cost to your wife of moving the seat is nearly three times the inconvenience cost to you.

Why then, the continued controversy? Richard Harter, a (male) mathematician, has calculated the incremental costs of moving from bachelorhood or spinsterhood to connubial bliss. Since men sometimes need the seat down, they are used to bearing the cost of moving it. Women who live alone or with other women need never move the seat at all; therefore the incremental costs of moving to a mixed household are obvious.

Yet I feel that these thinkers have missed the bigger picture. Assume two types of man: the considerate gentleman and the selfish pig. It is famously difficult for women to distinguish them at first sight. Nevertheless it is easy for the gentleman to signal his 'type' by returning the lavatory seat to the horizontal. This is a profitable lesson and one that I learned early.

Yours, at the appropriate angle, The Undercover Economist

Dear Undercover Economist,

I want to pay someone to redecorate the kitchen, rather than slave over the paint pots myself – not only because I hate DIY but also, as a professional, I want my wealth to trickle down through society. However, my husband says we should all do our own manual work so that when the oil runs out we'll have the skills to tackle any job. What do you think?

– Marion de Berker, Bristol

Dear Mrs de Berker,

You are both confused. You will not create any 'trickle down' wealth if you decide to pay a professional decorator instead of working on your kitchen in your spare time. If you do it yourself, the money you would have paid to the decorators will instead be spent on holidays, restaurants or clothes. I am not sure why you think your decorator deserves the cash, rather than the waiter or the travel agent.

Perhaps you're afraid that if you don't hire a decorator the cash will be unspent for a while and nobody will benefit from receiving it.

But your restraint will free up resources for investment and future generations will be richer.

The reason to get the decorators in is that they'll do it better than you and it will take less time to earn the money to pay them than to do it yourself.

Meanwhile your husband shows signs of advanced paranoia. Send him away on a paintball weekend and have the decorators in while he's gone.

I don't know what things look like over in Bristol but here in London there are few indications that we are about to return to the stone age. Even if civilisation does come to an end, I am not sure why it will be so valuable to know how to redecorate your kitchen.

Yours apocalyptically, The Undercover Economist

Dear Undercover Economist,

I have a two-year-old daughter. I am thinking of making contributions into her tax-free 'Child Trust Fund' accounts to help with university fees or a deposit on her first home. The trouble is that under the rules of the scheme the money becomes my daughter's on her eighteenth birthday. There will be nothing I can do to prevent her blowing the cash on boyfriends, fast cars and fancy holidays. What can you advise?

– Timothy Molinari, Hackney

Dear Timothy,

You're clearly a man who likes to think ahead, as well as being a control freak. You could, therefore, look for other ways to invest money and give out the cash on your own terms. That would mean you would pay more tax or more fees, or perhaps both. But the fundamental truth is that such schemes will not prevent your daughter from living the high life if she wants to.

What you have failed to realise is that with cash from Daddy safely tucked into a trust fund to be accessed at age twenty-one or twenty-five or even thirty, your daughter can take the documentation to any bank and take out a loan at once.

What, then, to do? The obvious approach is to leave your money to Battersea Dogs and Cats Home and make it perfectly clear to your daughter and her bank manager that this is what you have done.

That should work but I am not sure why you have so little confidence in your daughter's ability to make her own decisions. Perhaps you should have bought a fast car yourself when you were younger – it would certainly have loosened you up a little. And, by the way, there is no way she will wait until she is eighteen to do foolish things with boyfriends.

Yours overcontrollingly, The Undercover Economist

Dear Undercover Economist,

I am being divorced. Since I will have less disposable income – due to higher living costs plus alimony – and since I want to stay married, must I conclude that I will be permanently worse off?

– Gerard Nichols, Maastricht, Holland

Dear Gerard,

Commiserations, it certainly doesn't look good. If it's any consolation, I can think of five Nobel laureates in economics with helpful suggestions.

It is probably best to start by measuring your 'permanent income', the term Milton Friedman used to describe average income over your lifetime. Your future permanent income, in monetary terms, does seem to have fallen, although Friedman's analysis argues that you should spread the misery over the rest of your life, rather than taking a big depressing hit all at once.

Gary Becker analyses the non-monetary returns to marriage. These are positive for you but clearly negative for your wife. Ronald Coase's ideas suggest the opportunity for negotiation: it might be that you like the marriage more than your wife dislikes it. If so you could pay her to stay married to you.

Failing that, you should look on the bright side. Robert Merton and Myron Scholes would suggest that you bear in mind the fresh options opened up by this divorce. They may not be obvious to you now but you may find yourself enjoying the opportunity to smoke in bed, flirt with impunity or even marry an heiress. This is all uncertain but the sheer randomness of life is what gives these options their value.

Friedman, Becker, Coase, Merton and Scholes all earned the Nobel Prize for their efforts. Going through a divorce is hell but there is always a little economics to cushion the pain.

Yours consolingly, The Undercover Economist

Dear Undercover Economist,

I am seventy-two and about to prepare my will. Knowing that some of my daughters have married well and the other will probably remain single (and therefore be financially disadvantaged in comparison), there seems to be a moral justification to be more generous to the latter. Observing that my unmarried daughter might be more likely to provide assistance to me in my old age, why should I not be more generous to her? I would, in economic terms, be repaying her for services (hopefully to be rendered) which her siblings will probably be either too busy, or too absorbed with their children, to offer. Please give me an economic justification for being more generous to my unmarried daughter.

– Tom Holden, Australia

Dear Mr Holden,

Let's deal with this one point at a time. Divorced women tend to take a financial hit while divorced men tend to be better off than they were when they were married. What does that tell you? You might think that it suggests divorce is bad for women, but it equally suggests that marriage is bad for them. Women must hate being married if they are willing to pay to get divorced. And men must like marriage since they would be richer if they walked out the door. So don't feel too sorry for your single daughter: her married sisters are probably praying for a chunk of inheritance so that they can afford to divorce their husbands.

A better justification is your unmarried daughter's expected contribution to your care in your dotage. Perhaps you should be a bit more explicit about the arrangement: why not offer to pay her by the hour to spend time clearing up after you? To be fair you should also pay the others if they come to visit. This method may produce a hidden benefit: you can switch to a competitive tender on the open market. You may find that your children are not low-cost providers at all.

Yours competitively, The Undercover Economist

121

Dear Undercover Economist,

My young children, aged five and eight, are driving me insane. I try to discipline them but they can be so wilful. At times I lose my temper and spank them. Is this wrong? What else can I try?

– Gill Harnsley, Chelsea

Dear Ms Harnsley,

Children are rational utility maximisers but they have a high discount rate and therefore a short time horizon. Small immediate punishments and rewards are the most efficient way to give them the right incentives to behave.

Parents have trouble making credible promises of future punishments. Rational children know they can ignore threats of punishment if you have a record of bluster.

These two facts together argue for the time-honoured tradition of a chart with stars and black marks. The immediacy of the reward or punishment outweighs the fact that it is, after all, just a mark on a bit of paper. The chart can be reinforced by tying pocket money to the number of stars minus the number of black marks. This is an objective, transparent policy framework that will make it harder for you to renege on your threats: if the black marks are there on the chart, you can hardly cough up the allowance at the end of the week.

There is no need to spank your children unless you are poor. This is not to hold poor parents to different standards, simply to recognise that if a family is not rich enough to pay a generous allowance then there is no financial threat available. The main alternative to withdrawing pocket money is spanking, which is free.

The economist Bruce Weinberg has found that very poor parents spank their children and withdraw allowances less frequently than other parents, even those of modest income. But if you can afford reasonable pocket money, then taking it away is all the punishment you need.

Yours non-violently, The Undercover Economist

Dear Undercover Economist,

I'm an ambitious woman in my mid-twenties, just starting what I hope will be a stellar career in business. But I also very much want to have at least one child. How long should I leave it?

– Ms E. Jones, West London

Dear Ms Jones,

Mothers seem to do worse in the labour market than women without children but that might not be simple cause and effect. For instance it might indicate that women who expected successful careers delayed having children, but the delay was not the cause of the success.

It all seems imponderable but it isn't. Amalia Miller, an economist at the University of Virginia, studied the timing of maternity and its effect on earnings. That effect is large: delay maternity by just one year and you can expect your career earnings to rise by 10 per cent, partly because you will work longer hours and partly because you will enjoy a better wage rate. For professionals like you, the wage effect is even higher.

These numbers strip out the effects of choice because they are all based on accidents. Professor Miller made three types of comparison. She compared women who became mothers at twenty-seven with those who became mothers at twenty-eight despite both groups using contraception and therefore not choosing the timing. She also compared women who successfully got pregnant at twenty-seven with women who tried at twenty-seven but did not succeed for a year; or women who miscarried at twenty-seven and then got pregnant again a year later. The women wanted the same date of pregnancy but bad luck intervened – and their careers benefited.

Professor Miller's results suggest that you should leave your pregnancy as late as you dare. Her methods remind you, though, that you may not get to decide.

Yours fecundly, The Undercover Economist

Dear Undercover Economist,

My wife and I are about to have a new baby girl and we were planning to call her 'Aisha', which we think is a beautiful African name. The trouble is, we're not African and my mother-in-law has been agitating for something a bit more conventional, such as 'Molly' or 'Liz'. Can you recommend a course of action?

– Tim Monks, London

Dear Mr Monks,

First, would an African name cause your daughter to suffer discrimination in the workplace? Second, will she like the name on its own merits?

When the economists Sendhil Mullainathan and Marianne Bertrand sent out thousands of fake job applications to employers in Boston and Chicago, adding distinctively black or white names at random, they found unmistakable evidence of racial discrimination against the black-sounding candidates. And well-qualified black-sounding candidates did no better than poorly qualified black-sounding candidates. It's as though the employers just moved on whenever they came across a Jermaine or a LaTonya.

Yet other research by economists Roland Fryer and Steven Levitt suggests that giving a black child a white-sounding name does not help the child's prospects. What that implies in your rather rare situation is not clear but at least you will confuse the racists.

Then there is the question of your daughter's preferences. Teenagers want boring names but many adults feel differently. Thus you need to build flexibility into the full name: an interesting middle name with a tedious first name, and vice versa. She can vary them as time goes by, and I think she is more likely to get the decision right than you, me or even your mother-in-law.

Yours unconventionally, The Undercover Economist

Dear Undercover Economist,

My stepfather is an alcoholic and spends his time and money on nothing but self-intoxication. This results in me experiencing great anger and wanting to do something stupidly aggressive.

My mother has less and less money to run the house. I no longer live there but will soon have to contribute money to prevent my mother entering a downward spiral of debt. How do I control an alcoholic who is content only with a bottle in his hand? How do I solve the financial problem? How do I stop myself becoming wound up by my stepfather's actions?

– Name and address supplied

Dear Anonymous,

Your stepfather is addicted to alcohol but your real problem is that your mother is addicted to your stepfather and you are addicted to her. There are economic ideas about how to break an unwanted addiction (Nobel laureate Thomas Schelling coined the phrase 'egonomics') but they presuppose that the addict wants to kick the habit. It does not sound as if any of you actually wishes to break his or her respective addiction, which would make them 'rational addictions', as theorised by Gary Becker, another laureate, and Kevin Murphy. Taking into account all the costs and benefits, each of you would prefer to stay addicted.

You should therefore not be focusing on addictions but externalities. Your stepfather is imposing a grievous cost on you and your mother but not offering any compensation. Ronald Coase – yet another laureate – suggested that externalities could be bargained away. You could just pay your stepfather to stop drinking or he could pay you to stop complaining about it. The problem is that Coase's theorem requires that you are able to negotiate without costs in time, trouble or embarrassment. In your case, alas, this seems unlikely.

Yours, The Undercover Economist

Dear Undercover Economist,

I cannot help being fair when giving presents or rewards, even though I may actually want to give differently or the recipients may in fact deserve differently. I only differentiate between groups (my children, my nephews and nieces, my friends, etc.), but not within each group. Not wanting to show favouritism or cause rivalry, I give a present of equal value to every member of a group.

Were businesses to follow my example such 'incentives' would no longer serve as a motivating tool. But then this could also mean no ill feelings or disharmony, right?

– Aidida Rosenstock, Germany

Dear Aidida,

I am not sure why you think there would be so much harmony in a workplace where lazy, incompetent and rude workers are paid the same as the industrious, capable and affable. Still, you have a point. Research on competitive pay schemes shows that workers are indeed motivated by them – taking fewer days off, for example. But they also encourage staff to stab colleagues in the back by refusing to share equipment. Employers must judge whether the motivation for self-improvement outweighs the damage caused by poor teamwork.

I am more interested in why you adopt such odd principles yourself. Are you truly indifferent to whether your children become beach bums or bankers? The right incentives could work wonders.

Even if all that matters to you is fairness, you should pay attention not to how much you yourself give but to how much each child – or friend – has after the gift has been given. The millionaire and the pauper receive the same from you, which means you are defining 'fair' from an egocentric standpoint. No doubt this minimises your own effort and embarrassment. How selfish.

Yours, in outrage, The Undercover Economist

Dear Undercover Economist,

My mother-in-law can be extremely aggravating and on a recent visit she managed to wind me up so badly that I made an unprintable remark to her. The fact that she fully deserved my outburst does not seem to carry much weight with her, nor my beloved wife. So things are now a little tense. I suppose I should apologise but I don't

want to encourage her nagging, nor acknowledge that
she was right (she wasn't). Can economics provide a
solution?

– James, North London

Dear James,

Economics is not the obvious starting point since an apology
appears to be what an economist would call 'cheap talk' – it costs
nothing and should therefore be meaningless. But help is at hand
from economist Benjamin Ho of the Stanford Graduate School
of Business. Ho has been conducting doctoral research on the
economics of apologies.

He begins with the observation that apologies make us more
likeable but also make us seem incompetent – an intuitive
response backed up by psychological research. For example the
psychologists Fiona Lee and Lara Tiedens showed subjects some
edited footage of Bill Clinton talking about the Lewinsky affair.

After viewing the clips in which Clinton seemed apologetic,
the subjects said they liked him more but respected him less. This
suggests that an apology is not cheap talk at all: it represents a
choice to appear loveable but bumbling. The alternative is to
admit nothing and look like a competent hard-man.

Your refusal to apologise sends a clear signal that you would be
pleased if your mother-in-law respected you but kept her distance. That sounds accurate, but you wonder why your wife is
upset?

Yours apologetically, The Undercover Economist

Dear Undercover Economist,

My wife and I have separated. Naturally our relationship is not great but it's OK. Now divorce proceedings have started and we will be dividing up our assets. Should I hire a lawyer? I am not convinced that it is worth the expense.

– Seth, via email

Dear Seth,

You have obviously grasped that this is a zero-sum game with two to four players. The assets will be divided between you, your soon-to-be-ex-wife, and any lawyers the two of you bring on board.

I can sympathise with your suspicion that the lawyer is money down the drain.

It is worth considering the scant evidence available.

The Austrian economist Martin Halla has collected data from divorce proceedings in his home country and he finds a curious pattern. Husbands end up paying the smallest alimony when no lawyers are involved. If the husband hires a lawyer but his wife does not, the alimony payment rises (and then there are fees to be paid, too). If the wife hires a lawyer or the couple hires a joint lawyer, the husband forks out still more. Worst-case scenario for hubby is if both sides hire their own lawyer. On top of that the proceedings are longer and more expensive.

Interpret that result with caution because it is not clear whether the lawyers cause poor settlements for husbands or whether husbands hire lawyers when things look grim. Still, the pattern that Halla discovered does bolster your scepticism.

In the absence of better information, then, Halla's research suggests that you have a dominant strategy, meaning one that is best no matter what your wife does. That strategy is not to hire a lawyer. And for goodness' sake, don't let your wife see any research from Martin Halla.

Yours covertly, The Undercover Economist

Dear Undercover Economist,

I feel guilty because I paid two hundred pounds to co-host a birthday party for my five-year-old with another mother but got at least three hundred pounds of gifts in return. As a guest I don't like these parties because you take two gifts in return for only one party bag. But co-hosting is surely a rational thing because you pay half and get a full complement of presents?

– South London Mum

Dear SLM,

Congratulations on your move to more efficient birthday parties. It seems to be a happy accident since you have failed to realise the true scarce resource here. It is not doggy bags or disposable toys but time. By hosting a joint party with a friend, you are saving time for many parents who would have had to attend two such parties in quick succession. The children may feel hard done by, but then again they may not. Even five-year-olds do not want a party every day.

As for making a profit on these parties, an economist understands that gifts need not be exchanged instantly and with exact accounting for value. You hosted a profitable party but feel exploited when others reciprocate – perhaps you should see these events as two sides of the same coin. It will not take long before these profits and losses even out. Surely the credit crunch is not so severe that you cannot wait a month or two for a return on your gift-giving?

As for the party bags, they are truly immoral: to quell your feelings of guilt you dose up other people's children with sugar and additives. Is this a generous act or a craven one? I commend your move to halve the supply of party bags; my only complaint is that you have not eliminated them altogether.

Yours, in celebration, The Undercover Economist

Dear Undercover Economist,

I gave my sister a 30 per cent share of my mortgage when buying a new house two years ago, in 2006, so she could get on the property ladder. In return she gave me some money towards the deposit on the house – about 20 per cent of the total put down. Given my larger share of the investment and commitment, should I get a greater proportion of the equity than my 70 per cent share if and when we sell?

– Ben

Dear Ben,

It is astonishing that you have entered into this enormously valuable contract without agreeing terms, but perhaps I should not be surprised – your letter suggests that you are unable even to think clearly.

You do not 'give' someone a share of a mortgage any more than you 'give' them a share of your restaurant bill.

If all you mean is that you gave her 30 per cent equity in exchange for a deposit, stick to the deal.

But I think you mean that your sister paid 20 per cent of your deposit and 30 per cent of your mortgage and has received nothing in return so far. You, on the other hand, have had your living costs subsidised and your risks in the property market hedged. Thanks to a housing bubble, your joint investment has paid off and you would now like to cream off some additional upside. Had there been a slump – widely forecast when you bought the house – would you be offering to bear more than 70 per cent of the loss?

There is no well-defined outcome from your befuddled arrangement but it would be reasonable for your sister to enjoy more of the upside.

She took on nothing but risk while you lived on the cheap. Family values indeed.

Yours, shocked, The Undercover Economist

———

Dear Undercover Economist,

I am twenty-two years old with a younger sister. My parents were pretty strict so I made sure I was a sensible teenager. I didn't sleep around, didn't take drugs, never seriously smoked and went on to a good graduate job. But now my seventeen-year-old sister is getting away with murder: my parents know she smokes, let her boyfriends stay overnight and turn a blind eye to other misdemeanours. It's just not fair. Did I make a mistake in being such a square as a teenager?

– Georgie H., Hertfordshire

Dear Georgie,

The latest *Economic Journal* presents a simple game-theory model of the problem. All teenagers wish to misbehave but fear parental sanctions. Parents wish to threaten punishment for transgressions but only some parents are strict enough to do so. Your younger sister's mere existence skewed the game to your disadvantage. Your parents are evidently soft-hearted, but had a clear incentive to pretend to be strict because every time they punished you they knew they were also deterring your sister.

Now that you have flown the nest the gains from 'acting strict' are much smaller and discipline has slipped. Your sister pushed and discovered that they did not push back; you would not have found it so easy. But sunk costs are sunk costs, so be content with your graduate job. And if you really want to take drugs and sleep around, I can assure you it is not too late.

Yours transgressively, The Undercover Economist

Dear Undercover Economist,

In some countries mothers and their newborn babies are kept in hospital for many days, while in others they are discharged quickly. Which is right? I'm pregnant and I want to know whether I should be lobbying for a long stay or for early release after my baby is born.

– Michelle, North London

Dear Michelle,

A simple analysis won't answer you because we would expect more complicated or worrying cases to stay longer in hospital. But that does not imply that long hospital stays cause complications and worry.

Instead we need to observe what happens to mothers and babies sent home early or late for no good reason.

Fortunately there is no shortage of such cases. Californian insurers will pay for a certain number of nights in hospital but the clock starts at midnight. A baby born at one minute past midnight has nearly twenty-four hours before clocking up one night in hospital; a baby born two minutes earlier will clock up her first night in hospital within seconds. The economists Douglas Almond and Joseph Doyle used such comparisons to examine whether the extra night was helpful.

They looked at whether mother and baby survived, and whether they had to be readmitted later. There was no evidence that longer hospital stays were helpful.

My experience is that an extended stay for mother and baby is a welcome respite – for the father.

Yours, in relaxation, The Undercover Economist

Dear Undercover Economist,

My husband and I both have fairly demanding jobs, and we also have two children under the age of five. Bedtime is sometimes fulfilling but more often exhausting and aggravating. Most of the work – especially the stories and the staring at the ceiling waiting for the children to fall asleep – is best done alone. So how should we share the chore?

Taking it in turns seems obvious but what about when one partner is particularly tired already? Should we be holding an auction or something?

– Sophie Jamieson

Dear Sophie,

Your problem is surprisingly subtle. Simply taking turns is inefficient since that may mean the wearier party being faced with the chore. But a more discretionary system of side-payments is complex, and may be corrupted if one of you feigns exhaustion when in fact you simply fancy a glass of wine and a bit of TV.

Such situations are common. For example a price-fixing cartel faces a trade-off between rigid profit-sharing rules and complex schemes to trade market share. The general problem has been analysed in the formidably mathematical research of Professor Susan Athey. She finds that less efficient but simpler schemes often – but not always – pay off. So you should indeed take turns and if that is occasionally sub-optimal, tough luck.

Please note that Athey also has two children under the age of five.

Yours alternately, The Undercover Economist

Dear Undercover Economist,

I am the mother of two young children and extremely grateful to my own parents for looking after them for a few hours now and then. My problem is that they stuff the kids with chocolates, crisps and ice-cream. This is not good for the children, their behaviour and my own efforts to feed them something nutritious. Why do the grandparents have such a different philosophy and can I do anything to change their thinking?

– F.M., Cumbria

Dear F.M.,

The symptoms are familiar but you have misdiagnosed the cause. Your parents do not have a different philosophy; they have different incentives. As you surmise, the costs of the junk-food strategy are mostly long-term: the children become fat, their teeth rot and they refuse to eat more wholesome fare.

In contrast the benefits – delighted smiles, grateful kisses, compliant silence – are all short-term. Their strategy is perfectly rational for temporary carers.

Rather than reasoning with your parents, you must change their incentives. Unfortunately this is not easy. You could try to bribe your parents but threats will be useless because they are doing you a favour.

Perhaps your best bet is to try to arrange for longer bouts of childcare. Your parents will have a fresh perspective on the merits of carrots after trying to put a three-year-old to bed in the midst of a sugar high.

Yours nutritively, The Undercover Economist

Dear Undercover Economist,

My young son came home from school and asked me: 'Mummy, what's a credit crunch?' How can I explain this to a five-year-old?

– Ms L.G., London

Dear Ms L.G.,

Once upon a time, not so far from the year of 2008, there was a blameless girl called Consumerella, who didn't have enough money to buy all the lovely things she wanted. She went to her Fairy Godmother, who called a man called Rumpelstiltskin who lived on Wall Street and claimed to be able to spin straw into gold. Rumpelstiltskin sent the Fairy Godmother the recipe for this magic spell. It was written in tiny, tiny writing so she did not read it but hoped the Sorcerers' Exchange Commission had checked it.

The Fairy Godmother carried away armfuls of glistening straw-derivative at a bargain price. Emboldened by the deal, she lent Consumerella – who had a big party to go to – 125 per cent of the money she needed. Consumerella bought a bling-bedizened gown, a palace and a Mercedes – and spent the rest on champagne.

The first payment was due at midnight. At midnight Consumerella missed the first payment on her loan. (The result of overindulgence, although some blamed the pronouncements of the Toastmaster, a man called Peston.) Consumerella's credit rating turned into a pumpkin and Rumpelstiltskin's spell was broken. He and the Fairy Godmother discovered that their vaults were not full of gold but ordinary straw.

All seemed lost until Santa Claus and his helpers, men with

implausible fairy-tale names such as Darling and Bernanke, began handing out presents. It was only in January that Consumerella's credit card statement arrived and she discovered that Santa Claus had paid for the gifts by taking out a loan in her name. They all lived miserably ever after. The End.

How to Fool a Wine Snob
Food, Drink and Entertainment

Good food and good wine, laughter and leisure: they may not be matters of life and death but as sources of joy and anxiety these things are rarely trivial. Lacking guidance, the task of choosing the right bottle of wine to bring to a dinner party can provoke indecision, shame and resentment. Coping with a shared refrigerator in a student house becomes a torment worthy of the fourth circle of hell.

The full toolbox of economics, from surveys to experimental research to high theory, is deployed here to answer these letters about how we pass the time together.

One of the great strengths of economics in such cases is that economists try to identify the universal principles at work. A typical advice columnist will tend to fuss over the specifics of a particular case. That is all very well for satisfying the prurience of the reader but little use when it comes to laying out advice that will apply in more than one circumstance. Economists have always been content to sacrifice specifics for the sake of an overarching theory, a Platonic idealisation of the problem at hand. 'Dear Economist' is no exception. And for the correspondents who receive such advice? There have been few complaints.

Dear Uncercover Economist,

Maximising one's skiing enjoyment should be a simple calculation involving the length and quality of ski run (S), divided by the time queuing for the ski-lift (Q). Unfortunately Q can be greatly lengthened by the French (F), who seem able to use barely perceptible spaces to travel at exactly twice the average speed of the queue (QvF). I would appreciate your thoughts on how I too can achieve QvF.

– Simon Jenner

Dear Mr Jenner,

Economics is about more than formulae. Your focus on petty mathematics, and petty queue-jumpers, is distracting you from the fact that the entire conundrum is a great money-making opportunity.

Economics is the study of the allocation of scarce resources. The ski-lift is such a resource and can be allocated efficiently or inefficiently. The queue is a simple, commonplace and grossly inefficient rationing mechanism.

An auction would be far more efficient. Imagine two adjacent lifts, one that auctions off spaces depending on demand to ensure that there are no queues; the other free of charge but attracting a substantial queue. Given that skiers can choose either lift, the waiting time on one and the price on the other will adjust until new skiers are indifferent between the two lifts. At this equilibrium both ski-lifts inflict the same cost on skiers.

However, the lift with the queue imposes a cost that is pure social waste: nobody benefits because people are queuing. The lift with the auction transfers the cost from the skiers to the ski-lift owner.

You now have all the information necessary to exact your revenge on the French. Set up a pay-per-lift and watch their euros roll in. Even the wily French cannot escape the laws of economics.

Yours, in the spirit of European cooperation,
The Undercover Economist

Dear Undercover Economist,

My close circle of friends follow a scheme of 'tour accounting', the basis of which is that we never really bother who pays the bill because, as we plan to remain friends for a lifetime, it will work out in the long run.

Is this sensible economically?

– Ruth Kirby, Surrey

Dear Ms Kirby,

Your inventive scheme mixes high risks with high rewards. The rewards are twofold: first, a massive saving on transaction costs. The late humorist Douglas Adams, who surely could have been an economist, theorised that the calculations involved in splitting a restaurant bill were so nonsensical as to deserve their own branch of surreal mathematics called 'Bistromathics'. Your system means that the waiter need not swipe a dozen credit cards for each meal and that you and your friends need never bother themselves with Bistromathics.

Second, each time a person picks up the bill she is sending a signal that she expects to be in the friendship long enough to be paid back. Life with your friends is an endless sequence of credible signals of friendship – a real love-in for the economically literate. Sadly you are making a mistake common to many junior game theorists: the equilibrium you describe is unstable in the face of entry. Pseudo-friends have an incentive to join your group, freeload on its generosity until challenged, and then walk away in debt to the tune of several meals.

Your only rational response is to require any new friends to pay a substantial deposit when they join your circle. Their early obligations could be paid out of the deposit, which would be forfeited in the event of non cooperative behaviour. Such a scheme will ensure that excess entry is not a problem that will trouble your circle of friends.

Your resident Bistromathematician, The Undercover Economist

Dear Undercover Economist,

Will somebody please explain to me the behaviour of my twelve-year-old daughter? Every moment seems to bring some new craze. It was Justin Timberlake; now it's

Madonna. Can I do anything to persuade her to make her own decisions rather than join some irrational herd of pre-teens?

– Tom Jacobs, Winchester

Dear Mr Jacobs,

Youthful 'crazes' may not be as crazy as you think. You describe an 'irrational herd' but what if the herd was perfectly rational?

Your daughter surely has her own opinion about the merits of, for instance, Mr Timberlake. Yet she realises that other girls hold valuable information about his strengths and weaknesses, and the listening pleasure afforded by rival entertainers. It would be foolish to ignore this information.

Rationally your daughter will observe the music chart and real-time information such as the popularity of the songs on file-sharing software or celebrity trackers such as the BBC's 'Celebdaq'. (Madonna is up 0.17 per cent over the past hour at the time of writing.) Each person who downloads a Madonna track confirms the quality of the music. The result can be a chain reaction as more people download or, if no one follows the lead of these early adopters, it can be a flop.

An economically illiterate observer, such as the father of a music fan, might observe frenzies and crashes in the popularity of artists. He would not realise they were the result of each girl making sophisticated inferences about the information held by the others. Your daughter is clearly a gifted economist.

I recommend that you study the subject yourself. Not only would you understand your daughter better than before, you might even gain an appreciation of Madonna.

Yours, a rational herd animal, The Undercover Economist

Dear Undercover Economist,

My favourite table at the local pub is getting too
crowded. A few of us sit down for a few drinks, then, as
the stragglers come and join us one by one, there's
hardly room to bend your elbow. Why does this happen
and what can we do about it?

– George Pollitt, Buckinghamshire

Dear Mr Pollitt,

How fortunate for your landlord, but I can see why you are irri-
tated. It is easy enough to diagnose the cause of your problem
with the help of Steven Salop's 'circular city' model of differenti-
ated competition under free entry. His analysis is a classic of
1970s industrial economics.

In Salop's model, firms compete in a circular space – think of
ice-cream vendors located around the edge of a boating lake.
Salop shows that each of these firms imposes costs on the others
(by poaching customers), so you reach a point where there is too
much entry.

What better explanation of your own plight? You sit around a
pub table, and each new drinker decides whether or not to
squeeze in and join you. Yet of course they do not consider the
impact on everybody else's comfort. The final person to join you
(before others decide they would rather stand) only just prefers
sitting down to standing up. He might as well stand. Of course
everyone who must make space for him is far from indifferent.

The solution is simplicity itself – and it is also a tradition that I
am surprised you are not upholding. Each new companion should
pay an entry fee in compensation to the others – traditionally one
pint per person. This elegant solution ensures that incumbent

drinkers are compensated for giving up space. It also ensures that the more crowded the table is, the less tempting it is to join it.

Your round, The Undercover Economist

Dear Undercover Economist,

From time to time I go out with friends to a restaurant. Frequently someone suggests: 'Why don't we order a number of different dishes and share them?' I do not like this idea (because it is messy and it dilutes the pleasure of choosing), but once the suggestion is made it seems churlish and anti-social to object. How can I break this cycle while retaining my friends?

– Mr K., Dublin

Dear Mr K.,

I feel the same way. Why should I be obliged to trade my rare steak for some fool's chicken Kiev? Still, there is more to this than simply finding a polite way to object.

The difficulty – insoluble at first sight – is that while you dislike the fuss, other people enjoy having their meals chopped up like baby food. Sharing should occur if your irritation at the practice is outweighed by their delight; and should not occur otherwise. Who is to make this judgement?

Fortunately the Coase theorem, developed by the revered economist Ronald Coase, predicts a happy outcome if property rights are clearly specified. Rather than refuse outright, you should insist that each person holds ownership rights over the dish they order. Mutually agreed trades are of course permissible. This should ensure that splitting dishes occurs only when socially efficient, and you will not be obliged to participate, although an excellent offer of compensation may persuade you to do so.

According to the Coase theorem, your problem until now has been that property rights over dishes have been vague.

I should caution you that the theorem does not hold if the costs of holding discussions are high. Economists often fret that 'It's not easy to get all the negotiators around the table.' Given the context, that should be the least of your worries.

Yours efficiently, The Undercover Economist

Dear Undercover Economist,

I recently bought a collectible comic book on eBay. The seller had a perfect feedback rating but the book is in far worse condition than he claimed. I am now inclined to post a negative comment – but maybe this is too harsh. Also, I am afraid of retaliation. What would you recommend?

– Jim Hertz, California

Dear Jim,

Let the world know that this guy is a fraud. As most readers will know, eBay is a vast internet-based car boot sale, where people buy and sell all kinds of goods from each other using auctions. After each transaction the buyer and seller publicly rate each other.

This is supposed to encourage honest behaviour but, perhaps because of the doubts you express, 199 out of 200 ratings are positive.

Economists Patrick Bajari and Ali Hortacsu recently surveyed the economic literature their brethren have produced about eBay. They report that you are right to expect retaliation; nearly half of negative ratings are reciprocated. But are you right to fear it?

As far as we economists can tell, eBay sellers enjoy a premium if they collect hundreds of positive ratings; but one or two negative comments do not cause much harm. This makes some sense: after all, it is hard to fake hundreds of satisfied customers.

Negative comments do have one clear effect, though: they make it more likely that subsequent negative comments will be posted quickly. Apparently some sellers are behaving badly but nobody wants to be the first to say so. By opening the floodgates you will do other eBay users a favour. And if this really is just a one-off, the seller will not suffer. Meanwhile his retaliatory comment will not harm your own dealings – unless you have a queue of dissatisfied customers just waiting for an excuse to say so.

Yours vengefully, The Undercover Economist

———————

Dear Undercover Economist,

I find that increasingly my decisions are being made based on 'rankings' of a sort. I choose recipes from epicurious.com based on the number of forks each

recipe has received. I check my books on Amazon.com
to see how many stars they received. But I'm worried
that these rankings are self-perpetuating. How can I
choose better recipes and read better books?

– Tim Bartlett, New York

Dear Mr Bartlett,

Your trust in other people's taste is touching and may occasionally
be sensible. James Surowiecki's recent book, *The Wisdom of
Crowds*, has made famous the fact that some problems, such as
guessing the weight of an ox, are better solved by averaging the
guesses of a large number of people than by asking a farmer.

The wisdom of crowds applies only to common-value problems, where the answer is an objective truth. Collective wisdom
about a recipe means nothing unless we are all questing after the
Platonic form of a recipe for ratatouille; but if so, the more opinions we seek, the closer we will get.

Unfortunately, as you recognise, a recipe may be popular simply
because people choose from the ranking tables. A better ranking
system would not allow people to see the list of popular items until
they had made their own choices, and would discount heavily any
choices then made by clicking on the 'most popular' charts.

Otherwise the wisdom of crowds is obscured by 'herding' behaviour: when you log into Amazon.com you decide that whatever your
prior beliefs about the virtue of Harry Potter might be, eighteen billion fans can't be wrong. Because you rely on the opinions of others,
your choice reveals no new information and the rest of us do not get
to benefit from whatever insight you might have had. Since you are
evidently the quintessential blank slate, this may be no great loss.

Yours popularly, The Undercover Economist

Dear Undercover Economist,

I'm planning to take a sabbatical to travel around the world with my partner for eight months. But we have a dilemma: should we cut our trip short after four months and return to England for a best friend's wedding? It would mean that we would miss out on New Zealand (and four more months off work) – but maybe it would be worse to miss the wedding?

– Paula Marvin, London

Dear Paula,

Your choice would be simple if one of these plans was Pareto-superior to the other.

A Pareto-superior plan is one that makes at least one person better off and, critically, makes nobody worse off.

I can only presume that your best friend would prefer you to attend her wedding, while it's perfectly obvious that your partner would rather cavort in the antipodes for another four months. There is no way to make one of them better off without making the other worse off, so unfortunately neither option is Pareto-superior.

How, then, are you to choose?

I recommend the Hicks-Kaldor compensation test. If you could (in principle) offer your best friend enough cash to assuage her feelings for your absence, and still feel that you were ahead on the deal, then the Hicks-Kaldor test is satisfied and you should stay the course for eight months.

Fortunately you do not actually need to bribe your friend to excuse you from the wedding – which is good news since the bribe might be misinterpreted. All you need to know is that four months of fun and frolics together for you and your partner is worth more than the fleeting pleasure your friend will get at noticing you amid the crowds at her wedding. Put like that, your choice is obvious.

Your Pareto-superior, The Undercover Economist

Dear Undercover Economist,

My new year's resolution was to get more exercise so I joined a gym. I'm embarrassed to say that I've hardly been. I have the option to cancel the membership, but perhaps I should keep it as an incentive to get fit?

– Janet Taggart, Glasgow

Dear Janet,

Many health clubs offer three types of membership. There is the option for the infrequent visitor – a pass entitling you to, say, ten visits. Then there is a monthly membership that continues indefinitely until cancelled. This is handy for regulars who may have to move or travel and so want the option of cancelling. There is also annual membership which lapses if not renewed: this is cheaper per month but less flexible.

Different contracts suit different people but we almost invariably pick the wrong one. For example the monthly contract is favoured by people like you who don't actually show up to the gym. Worse, those hapless suckers are too lazy even to cancel the contract, meaning that many of them would have been better off even had they signed up for a year and never gone. (This insight comes from an excellent paper titled 'Paying Not to Go to the Gym', by economists Stefano DellaVigna and Ulrike Malmendier. Bridget Jones features in the bibliography.)

My recommendation is for you to see if you can switch to a pay-per-visit pass. This will work out cheaper unless you experience a startling change of willpower. (If you do you can always get annual membership later.) If you're looking for financial motivation, why not instead make a bet of a thousand pounds that you will go to the gym every day for the rest of the year? I'm ready to take your money any time.

Yours healthily, The Undercover Economist

Dear Undercover Economist,

When I go to a restaurant a dish that costs more to make – perhaps lobster or the product of an expensive chef's imagination – costs more to purchase. The same is true when I go to a clothes store.

However, when I go to see a movie at my local cinema, no matter what the film, no matter how much it cost to make, it costs the same to see.

As I only go to big-budget flicks that have been praised to the rafters, I feel I am being subsidised by the poor folks who are watching cheap run-of-the-mill pictures. Why don't movie theatres have adjustable pricing?

– Arthur Spirling, Rochester, NY

Dear Mr Spirling,

You are confused. You are not consuming a film but a film screening, and film screenings cost the same to produce no matter what is in the projector. The price of producing the film in the first place is irrelevant.

Nevertheless there is a puzzle here. While we shouldn't expect big-budget films to command higher ticket prices, these prices should surely vary in an attempt to get every seat in the house full. It's not obvious that popular movies should be more expensive: the most popular books tend to enjoy the greatest discounts. But completely uniform pricing is odd.

One explanation is that people might buy a cheap ticket and then sneak into a more expensive screening; but uniform pricing predates the multiplexes. A second explanation, advanced by economist Barak Orbach, is that distributors don't like to be associated with 'discount movies' and so they tell cinemas what price to charge. Since this is illegal in the US, their instructions have to be simple, hence uniform pricing. I prefer the simplest explanation: cheap tickets with minimum confusion is a great way to sell popcorn.

Yours uniformly, The Undercover Economist

Dear Undercover Economist,

From time to time I find myself eating a meal with an unlimited supply of food: sometimes an all-you-can-eat buffet, sometimes a more sophisticated meal laid on by a friend or someone trying to impress: weddings, banquets, that kind of thing. I like food but there are limits to how much I can eat. So how should I pace myself for optimal enjoyment of the meal?

– Mr M. Newman, Shrewsbury

Dear Mr Newman,

This turns out to be a surprisingly deep problem and naturally the optimum strategy will also depend on your tastes. (If you are concerned about your weight, fill up on Perrier, celery and lettuce; better yet, stay away from all-you-can-eat buffets.) Nevertheless I think there are some general principles here.

If the buffet offers you every choice simultaneously, your best strategy is to try a little of every plausible dish so that you can decide what you would really like to eat. Then go back and get properly stuck in: to your favourite dish if you have no taste for variety, otherwise to your favourite two or three.

If the dishes are presented sequentially, then you will have to take more risks. There is always the chance that you will take a too-small portion of what later turns out to have been much the best course.

Your best guide, then, is to consider the incentives of the food supplier. At a restaurant they will try to fill you with cheap stodge so hold back and wait for the good stuff to arrive. But at a wedding banquet they will try to make a good first impression. Guzzle the champagne and tuck into the starter: it will all fall apart from there. You do not want to be filling up on slices of wedding cake.

Yours, replete, The Undercover Economist

A friend of mine was recently in Mumbai where many pirated books from the West were on sale on the street. Along with Harry Potter, there was *The Undercover Economist*, priced at 3.95 rupees.

It was clearly a counterfeit – it is printed on inferior paper and smells rather gratifyingly of printer's ink. Knowing that it was a breach of copyright, should my friend have bought the book, thus aiding and abetting a criminal act and depriving you of your royalty? And after my friend had bought it, should I have accepted the gift? And having accepted and read it, should I send you your royalty payment? I have the book and cannot find the chapter which answers this.

– Christopher Hird, London

Dear Mr Hird,

Faced with this kind of illegal competition, the publishers tend to move upmarket, offering higher prices and higher quality and presuming that they will not be able to beat the counterfeiters on price. (The illicit copy cost about five pence – less even than my miserly royalty.) Those with scruples lose out, as do I and the publishers.

But that can hardly be your concern. Even though the cheap version is inferior, it is a similar product. You did not, for instance, miss out on the 'official' discussion of piracy because it's not in the legal edition either. So you and your friends cannot be blamed for breaking the law and buying the illicit version.

It is kind of you to offer to send a royalty payment. If you are going to do things properly, though, you should also compensate the publishers and printers for their lost income, which is no less

157

hard-earned. Since you saw fit to send me photographic evidence of your crime along with your email address, perhaps this would be your wisest course.

Yours, from the original, The Undercover Economist

———————

Dear Undercover Economist,

An offer recently came up for me to buy, for fifty pounds, a discount card that halves the bill at many London restaurants. Three friends agreed to contribute equally to the cost and go out to a favourite restaurant, knowing that we would save more than this.

I got the card and booked the restaurant. Everything went fine until the end of an excellent meal. We had saved fifty-eight pounds. But the other three only grudgingly handed over their £12.50 to me.

They felt they had ended up just buying me a free card. I thought the expectation was that since I went to the trouble of setting it up, and they had saved money, they would thank me for my efforts.

– Martin Haigh, London

Dear Mr Haigh,

You have only yourself to blame both for being so vague about the terms of the deal and for being so niggardly when you divided the gains.

After they paid you for the meal and the card, each of your friends saved two pounds and the trouble of booking a restaurant, while you saved fifty-two pounds, of which fifty pounds went towards your discount card. It is true that that is a gain for all of you but it is an uneven gain.

Experiments in economic psychology have shown that most people would rather have no deal at all than accept a tiny gain while watching a fat cat guzzle the cream. Had you been a stranger rather than a friend, your dining companions would have simply refused your outrageous demands.

You should have been both more specific and more generous.

Telling your friends you planned to charge them fifty pounds just for booking a restaurant would at least have spared you all this embarrassing evening.

Yours frankly, The Undercover Economist

Dear Undercover Economist,

I regularly have dinner with a friend, alternating between his house and mine. My difficulty is that he is a wine snob. He is always puffing about the expensive wines he brings over to my place and is then sniffy about the offerings I take round to his. I don't know much about wine and I cannot afford to satisfy his taste for fancy vintages. This is starting to spoil what are supposed to be pleasurable evenings. Please help.

– Oliver Morris, South London

Dear Mr Morris,

I sympathise with your plight, being a penny-pinching wine duffer myself. A friend once handed me a wine guide and suggested that I consult it before I next brought a bottle round.

But I now have a resource unavailable to the ordinary citizen: the newly published *Journal of Wine Economics*. The first edition of the journal confirms what I have long suspected: wine is a racket.

An analysis of wine prices by two French researchers shows that prices are driven by the label on the bottle, which gives the year and the origin of the wine. The fact that one wine is rated as excellent and another as mediocre by a panel of experts in a blind taste test makes very little difference to the price.

The authors comment, 'As the jury grade seems a priori a reasonable measure of quality, one might have expected this variable to have a more important influence on prices.'

If the label is all that matters, a simple strategy suggests itself. Steam the labels off the empty bottles he leaves at your place and attach them to the bottles you take when it is your turn to go round to him. Since, according to the *JWE*, most people actually prefer cheaper wines in blind tests, you may even be doing him a favour.

Yours blindly, The Undercover Economist

Dear Undercover Economist,

I live in a student house with six others. All of us drink milk, some a lot, and some a little. Only three of us buy milk, and we buy three different varieties, meaning my preferred type can quickly run out.

Worse, my variety (semi-skimmed) seems to be the second preference of everyone else.

Free-riding is common but I don't want to spoil the atmosphere with strict rules and enforcement mechanisms. What course of action would you recommend?

– Haakon, Oxford

Dear Haakon,

You clearly think that people would never volunteer their fair share of the milk bill and that the monitoring systems necessary to ensure compliance would be onerous. This is a naive reading of economic theory because even rational economic agents can gain utility from acting honestly. Your course of action therefore needs to be identified empirically.

Draw inspiration from Paul F., also known as 'the bagel man'. Paul F. is a retired economist who now runs a bagel delivery business to offices. He operates an honour system, where people take bagels and leave the cash to pay for them.

Paul F. keeps scrupulous records about the payment rates of all his clients and shared them with Steven Levitt and Stephen Dubner, the authors of *Freakonomics*.

Perhaps you should simply leave a contribution box to make it easy for your housemates to contribute a few pennies as they swipe your milk. Paul F. found that this system produced a payment rate of 89 per cent. Even better, he saw more honesty in small offices and in the office where he himself worked.

A student house is probably similar.

Honesty only broke down at times of stress, such as Christmas – so guard the box in exam season.

Yours honestly, The Undercover Economist

Dear Undercover Economist,

I am often offered the chance to have an unauthorised copy of a current film downloaded from the web. As family circumstances presently preclude cinema trips, these offers present my only chance to see some films promptly.

I do not believe in enjoying the fruits of other people's labours for free. So is there any way in which I can make financial reparation for watching an unauthorised copy?

I live very close to a cinema so one option is to buy a ticket for a screening even though I won't actually be there. Or I could buy a copy of the DVD when it comes out, even though I don't really want to own it.

If I cannot put this right in economic terms, my conscience tells me not to watch!

– Yvonne, London

Dear Yvonne,

You should certainly watch since there is a positive benefit to you and zero marginal cost to the studio. Yet I believe you're right to feel uneasy about free-riding on someone else's time and talent. It is not only unfair but contributes to the wrong incentives for future film-making; in fact one suspects that the reason so many Hollywood blockbusters are childish is that the studios know adults don't have time to go to the cinema any more.

But your proposal to buy cinema tickets or DVDs doesn't seem right either. It sends a misleading signal that cinemas and

DVDs are what you want. You might try alternating your patronage of cinemas and DVDs, while downloading pirated copies many more times than you actually need to. If the studios are paying attention they might start to realise what it is you really want.

All this assumes that your need for an immediate copy is genuine.

I would question that. Do you shoplift when you're in a hurry?

Yours conscientiously, The Undercover Economist

Dear Undercover Economist,

When purchasing perishable food items I look for those that have the longest 'use by' date, even if I intend to consume them immediately. As a result I often bypass items that will be within their 'use by' date when I intend consuming them, in preference for items with an even longer shelf life. Can I be accused of being wasteful by not purchasing items with the shortest acceptable shelf life, since I am increasing the likelihood that they remain unsold?

– Andrew, London

Dear Andrew,

I hardly think the blame can be laid at your doorstep. The fault instead is with the unimaginatively static pricing on the part of the food retailers. They are presenting you with two different products at the same price and you are simply choosing the better, fresher offering.

It is true that if you plan to eat the food immediately the value you place on the fresher product might be lower than the value to someone who planned to buy it and leave it sitting around for a couple of weeks.

On the other hand many people don't check the dates because they don't care. It would be a shame if they got the fresher product at your expense.

Ideally, then, retailers would adjust their prices to reflect the staleness of the food, with the price declining very slightly over time, before being slashed as the 'use by' date approaches. Freshness fetishists like you would gladly pay more while students, pensioners and computer programmers would scoop up the cheapest products and scrape off the mould.

Products would be allocated efficiently according to preferences for freshness. It can only be a matter of time before the supermarkets catch on.

Freshly yours, The Undercover Economist

———

Dear Undercover Economist,

I'm a referee at the local basketball association. In one of the teams is a fantastic-looking woman. She is distractingly beautiful but also prone to committing fouls, often collecting the maximum of five fouls and being forced to be substituted.

Upon receiving her fifth foul, she nearly always walks to the bench, furiously removes her singlet and sits around for the remainder of the game in her sports bra. This brings the two male referees great utility.

However, it is costly to call for each of those five fouls. No referee wants the gorgeous girl to be angry with him, as we all hold on to the slim possibility that our stars may align one day.

Grasping this slim hope, sometimes each referee will avoid making fifty-fifty calls in the hope that his partner will. If both officials think this way too often, then she stays on court and so do her clothes. What to do?

– David

Dear David,

If you have even a slim chance with this woman, there is some benefit from letting the other referee call the foul. You simply need to collude by taking turns to make the tough call. Economics tells us that even though you have partially conflicting interests, when the situation is repeated again and again you can cooperate by the use of mutual threats. If the other ref doesn't do his share, you refuse to call any fouls until he does. This is called the, um, 'tit for tat' approach.

However, having read your letter I believe that is a hypothetical situation. Even if you never call another foul, you have precisely zero chance with this lady. Call fouls all you like because there's no way to make the situation worse.

Yours, tit for tat, The Undercover Economist

Dear Undercover Economist,

Having recently acquired a personal video recorder, I find myself using the time-shift facility when watching commercial TV.

I start watching a programme around fifteen minutes after it has commenced broadcasting – by doing this I am able to fast forward through the adverts. Am I breaking my 'contract' with the broadcaster by not watching its adverts and do I miss out on some products that might be of value to me?

– Paul, Dorset

Dear Paul,

If everybody did as you do, advertisers would give up and broadcasters would have to find a new source of income. That need not concern you, however. If you time-shift and others do not, no harm is done. And if they all time-shift, you'd be a fool to do otherwise, wouldn't you?

The more pertinent question is whether these adverts are worth your time. If you earn forty thousand pounds a year, then you make five pounds in the time it takes you to watch fifteen minutes of advertising. This is a rough guide to the opportunity cost of your time.

If the adverts are enjoyable or informative, perhaps that is a price worth paying but it seems unlikely. While an advertisement in the *Financial Times* might alert you to a sophisticated product, mainstream television adverts are more likely to remind you that actors can be paid to hold fizzy drinks or that when a car is filmed from a helicopter and driven by a stuntman along a remote mountain road, it looks rather cool.

I recommend, then, that you watch a few advertising breaks while keeping a running tally: the cost of time spent watching adverts versus your estimate of the benefits thus derived. I suspect you will find that time shifted is time saved.

Yours shiftily, The Undercover Economist

Dear Undercover Economist,

I am concerned at how violent films are these days and I think the censors should be much stricter in cutting out scenes of explicit violence. I was wondering if there is any support in economic theory for my view.

– A Concerned Parent, Kent

Dear Concerned Parent,

If I watch a splatter-fest and it causes me to punch somebody, that's about as good a definition of a negative externality as you can get.

The cinema doesn't care, unless a fight breaks out at the popcorn stand.

Nor do I. Only the poor chap with the broken nose feels differently about it all and his feelings are not going to be taken into account. Yet here economic theory would prescribe not censorship but a tax on violent films.

This argument assumes that the effect of a violent film is to provoke more violence. That is not clear. I understand that when people watch violent images in laboratory experiments they become more violent. (I'm not sure how this is measured: maybe a few psychologists were forced to eat their clipboards.)

But what you are not considering is this: when the local bully-boys are in the cinema watching *UltraDeath III: The Revenge*, they are not drinking lager or getting into fights. A new piece of research from economists Gordon Dahl and Stefano DellaVigna shows that when a violent film is on at the multiplex, violent crime falls during the evening and stays lower until the next morning. If a slushy romance is screened, the thugs go to the pub instead and mayhem ensues. Dahl and DellaVigna reckon violent films prevent 175 assaults a day in the US.

This suggests that if you plan on banning them, you might want to find a distracting alternative.

Yours violently, The Undercover Economist

Dear Undercover Economist,

I suffer ridicule from economist friends when visiting a local restaurant. The restaurant supplies complimentary tissues and toothpicks to customers. My friends freely use them and even take some for later use. I feel this is wasteful and not 'playing the game' but their arguments seem more logical – there's no extra cost to taking more, it is included in the costing for the meal, and I'm the mug subsidising everyone else. How can I overcome my hang-up and become a maximising consumer?

– Stuart

Dear Stuart,

This absurd pricing policy is, sadly, ubiquitous. But have you noticed that the right to sit at a restaurant table is also supplied free with the meal? Restaurants try to get around this by charging extra for goods that disproportionately lengthen the time spent at the table – starters, coffee, perhaps also wine. Why not try persuading your economist friends to linger for a few hours after your meal, just for the joy of consuming a free service? You might pass the time constructing miniatures from the toothpicks.

You have already realised that your friends are correct. Perhaps more persuasive than the pure logic is the knowledge that by grabbing tissues and toothpicks they are holding back the forces of communism. I dimly recall – but have not been able to confirm – that Lenin held up free condiments as an example of the way goods could be free and yet not rationed. It is up to right-thinking people to prove him wrong by walking off with the entire stock.

By grabbing toothpicks, your friends are chipping away not only at bits of salad but at the ideological foundations of communism. They deserve your support.

Yours with spotless teeth, The Undercover Economist

––––––––––––

Dear Undercover Economist,

As a keen silver surfer, I find YouTube an excellent way to revisit comedy favourites such as Monty Python and Peter Cook and Dudley Moore.

I feel guilty watching pirated material but what really puzzles me is why people post it for my delectation. Can you explain?

– O. Grizos

Dear O. Grizos,

It is a conundrum, I agree. Someone in possession of a vintage piece of sophisticated comedy – say, *Derek and Clive Get the Horn* – could simply spend his time watching it rather than posting it to the internet. The self-interested rational agent that populates some economic models would not behave like this.

The puzzle deepens when you consider the impressive achievements of the voluntary networks that have been enabled by the internet. Blogs are competing with online newspapers. Music-sharing networks have the record industry in a panic. Wikipedia needs no hype from me.

But while this behaviour may be economically and socially significant, most people participate only in the way you do – as consumers. J.K. Rowling's books attract thousands of reviews on Amazon. Yet the overwhelming majority of her readers – more than 999 in every thousand – don't bother to post a review. Frankly if 0.1 per cent of people make unrewarded contributions to the internet, that's just a rounding error away from nobody at all.

Economists love efficiency and it is not very efficient to produce an explanation of behaviour that hardly anyone engages in. I suggest, then, that you do the research yourself. Film your conclusions and we'll all watch them on YouTube.

Your free-riding correspondent, The Undercover Economist

In restaurants my husband always picks something better than me. It's boring to choose the same as him. What can I do?

– Sarah

Dear Sarah,

The behavioural economists Dan Ariely and Jonathan Levav speculated that we all tend, like you, to alter our choices to fit in with those around us – and they decided to put the theory to the test.

They came to an agreement with a local bar, dressed up as bar staff, and offered unsuspecting groups free samples from a choice of four tempting local beers. (One of the customers recognised Professor Ariely and assumed that his academic career had run aground.)

Sometimes the experimenters took the orders in conventional fashion; at other times they made each person's order confidential by asking them to write their desired beer on a piece of paper. After bringing the samples, Ariely and Levav noted how much the recipients had enjoyed their beers.

You will recognise your predicament in their results. First, when orders were called out publicly, people tended to avoid duplicating the choices of others. Second, that mattered: the people who chose first were significantly happier with their choices than those who felt obliged to choose whatever beer was left over. (This survey was done in the US. When transferred to Hong Kong, people instead tended to emulate the first choice. But, again, those who chose first were happier.)

The implication is obvious. You should make a mental note of what you wish to eat and not change your mind when your husband announces his selection. If that is too 'boring', the solution is even simpler: order first.

Yours independently, The Undercover Economist

Dear Undercover Economist,

I frequently extract large sums of money from Bozzer, my flatmate, in our regular poker game. He's convinced variance is to blame for his losses; in truth, however, he's simply terrible – and I'm simply delighted with my new watch. Am I right to exploit him in this way?

– R. Casablanca

Dear Mr Casablanca,

Unless you are holding poor Bozzer's family hostage in the basement, this is a voluntary transaction between consenting adults. Presumably he knows that he is losing money, even if he is not smart enough to work out why. And poker is lots of fun: even if he recognises that he is outclassed and the game is costing him, it may still be worth his while. After all, no customer makes a profit from going to the cinema either but we rarely worry about that.

On that basis you have no case to answer.

However, I cannot wholeheartedly give you the absolution you seem to be seeking. You must first establish whether Bozzer is a poker addict. I'll spare you the technical details – let's just say that they probably involve hyperbolic discounting – but I can recommend an approach for dealing with a rational addict. If, away from the card table, Bozzer says that he wishes he could quit the poker habit, you must help to discourage him. Perhaps you could enlist a third party to hold on to cheques from the pair of you. She would post the money to a charity if you are ever caught gambling together.

I must also warn you that things may not be as they seem. Is Bozzer, perhaps, playing the long game?

If one evening he suggests raising the stakes, beware.

You think he's the 'fish' – but he may be reeling you in.

Yours – and raise you, The Undercover Economist

Dear Undercover Economist,

Occasionally I buy and launch my own fireworks, generating cheerful positive externalities. Sadly some amateur launchings end in tragedy – and there is frequent talk of a private firework ban. What is the economically efficient way of dealing with those negative externalities?

– Jens Frolich Holte, Norway

Dear Jens,

If you've diagnosed the problem correctly, we can reach for a textbook solution. In a market with zero transaction costs, Coase theorem tells us that your neighbours could, in principle, pay you to hold firework displays, or not to, depending on their enjoyment of the spectacle or fear of injury.

More likely we would need to approximate the Coasian solution with an externality tax on fireworks (to reflect the risks) or a subsidy (to reflect the benefits). But I am not sure you have correctly identified the positive and negative externalities here.

Unless you are shooting the fireworks down the street, most of the risk is surely borne by you and your friends who've chosen to enjoy the display at close range.

There is no negative externality there: they've knowingly taken the risk.

On the positive externality side, I doubt that more distant neighbours enjoy the show as much as you think, not knowing when it is going to start. And they may be aggravated by the noise.

On balance where are the externalities?

We should focus instead on encouraging more responsible use of fireworks. If your firework display hurts an innocent, you should be liable. An appropriate level of likely damages will encourage you to take exactly the right amount of care with your displays.

Yours explosively, The Undercover Economist

Dear Undercover Economist,

When invited to dinner, I am often unsure whether to bring good wine. If I take an expensive bottle, it may go unappreciated – either through lack of appreciation or people not seeing what I've brought. Taking plonk means I can get a free ride on others' largesse, but my tight-fistedness could get rumbled – what do you recommend?

– Alex, Geneva

Dear Alex,

A simple bit of game theory will produce the optimal strategy. If this is a repeated interaction with people who know their wine, it's best to produce a good bottle. Reciprocity for your generosity will make this a good approach in the long run.

You will need to work out whether your dining partners do indeed understand wine. That is easy enough. Bring them something decent and see if they remark upon it. Then observe what they bring the next time you dine together. If your dinners are isolated invitations, or your hosts know nothing about wine, you may cheat with impunity. In short, vary your actions according to circumstance.

There is a deeper point here, though. You need to establish what is giving your fellow diners their utility – good wine or the pleasure of one-upmanship? My fellow columnist, the economist John Kay, points out that economists 'win' gift exchanges by spending less than everyone else, but most people 'win' gift exchanges by spending more.

If your fellow diners are economists, then my analysis will apply. Otherwise, as the sole economically minded diner, make sure your wine is a little less assuming than everyone else's. Everyone is happy, you save money and they feel smug. The moral: never forget to look for gains from trade.

Yours parsimoniously, The Undercover Economist

Email Scams, Odd Socks and the Existence of God
Miscellaneous Queries

Is it worthwhile to floss my teeth or drive to the recycling point? Should I take up smoking and if so what is the optimal age for the first puff? How much would be a fair price if China wanted to purchase Michigan? These and the other questions in this section might seem to be a miscellaneous selection.

Yet they do have something in common: that economics can be surprisingly human and wise. Take the penultimate letter of this collection, dealing with Joel Waldfogel's now-classic research paper, 'The Deadweight Loss of Christmas'. Waldfogel's paper is often interpreted as demonstrating the wastefulness of gifts, reinforcing the impression of economists as emotionally impoverished. In fact it demonstrates that it is more important to give something meaningful than to spend a lot of money – a surprisingly warm-hearted conclusion from the 'dismal science'.

But it shouldn't surprise us. Few people realise that 'dismal science' was an insult hurled by a racist, pro-slavery pamphleteer, Thomas Carlyle, who was frustrated that economists insisted on making fundamentally egalitarian assumptions. Economists tend to assume that everyone is equal and everyone is capable of making their own decisions. That clearly cannot be quite right but there are worse places to start.

So whether we are wondering about the value of a kiss, seeking to untangle the ethics of dwarf-tossing or figuring out how friends should divide a taxi fare, we will find there are solutions – or consolations – in economics.

Dear Undercover Economist,

I have bought a dilapidated house and hired some professional builders to renovate it. I thought I could ensure a good deal by soliciting a variety of quotes and estimates and choosing the lowest ones. But from the plumber to the decorators, every single tradesman has failed to stick to his estimate, renegotiated his quote or simply walked away without finishing the job. Can you advise?

– S.M., Bristol

Dear S.M.,

Your strategy has been, in effect, to hold a series of what economists call 'reverse auctions'. That is, rather than trying to sell for the highest price you are trying to buy for the lowest price. And it is to auction theory that you must turn for guidance.

Auction theorists have long recognised that when bidders have to estimate the value of a prize – whether the prize is a work of fine art, a licence to drill for oil or the obligation to rewire your electrics – then an auction will systematically select the most optimistic estimate.

Even if most bidders make accurate or even cautious estimates, there will usually be some who get it wrong – and one of them will of course win the auction. Winners of auctions tend to be disappointed, a phenomenon known as the 'winner's curse'.

When you are selling, you may be rather pleased that one bidder makes a mistake and accidentally offers too much. After all, all you need is to ensure that you get paid. But in a reverse auction it is hard to ensure that a disappointed winner will provide the promised service.

If the winning electrician discovers that he has bitten off more than he can chew, it will be difficult to hold him to his original quote. There is a long and dishonourable history of such renegotiations in the procurement business, so you are not alone.

You should certainly make sure that you get binding quotes in future, and to make sure they stick, withhold payment until the job is finished. But unless you are a skilled builder yourself, you may still find unpleasant surprises long after the event. My advice is to turn the winner's curse to your advantage. Why not sell the finished house at an auction?

Your bid, The Undercover Economist

Dear Undercover Economist,

My wife and I can never agree about buying extended warranties. She says they're a waste of money, I say better safe than sorry. Isn't it just a matter of opinion?

– R.A., Taunton

Dear R.A.,

Needless to say, your wife is quite right.

Any kind of insurance should always be a last resort.

Most people are risk-averse, meaning that they are willing to pay to avoid increased risk. If you have £1m, you would be right to turn down an offer to toss a coin for 'double or nothing' because the first million pounds is far more valuable to you than the second million.

But most insurance does not fall into that category. Over the course of your life you will earn hundreds of thousands of pounds, perhaps millions. A few hundred pounds here or there is inconsequential and nobody should accept insurance for such sums except on absolutely fair terms.

Most of us do not realise that we should insure only against losses that we truly cannot afford, such as large legal or medical costs, or simply watching our house burn down.

We get nervous about small risks, although if we put our insurance premiums into a savings account rather than giving them to an insurance company, we would be almost guaranteed to be well ahead in the long run.

Insurance companies are eager to take advantage of our ir-rationality, but competitive pressures tend to keep premiums at least somewhat fair. So the ideal way for an unscrupulous company to take our cash is to spring on us a surprise insurance deal linked to a purchase we have just made and therefore not subject to competition.

This is exactly what an extended warranty is. For a washing machine, a five-year warranty will cost about a hundred and fifty pounds but the fair value is about ten pounds. (A washing-machine repair costs about fifty-five pounds and the chance of a breakdown within five years is less than 20 per cent.) Incidentally your house insurance may well cover you in any case.

Put the hundred and fifty pounds in the bank instead. I suggest it goes into your wife's account: you are clearly not to be trusted with matters of high finance.

Your risk-neutral friend, The Undercover Economist

Dear Undercover Economist,

How do I choose the shortest queue at the supermarket?

– P.N., Aylesbury

Dear P.N.,

Mathematicians reckon the odds are against you. If you choose a queue at random, there will be a line on either side of you and thus a two-thirds chance that one will be faster.

Economists take a more sophisticated view. David Friedman, for instance, argues that the relevant discipline is financial market theory. Choosing the right queue is like picking the right portfolio of shares: if it were obvious which shares were good value, they wouldn't be good value any more. If it were obvious which queue would be quickest, everyone would join it. Naive attempts to 'beat the market' will fail.

Then there is the 'efficient markets' theory – you can't outperform a random choice of shares because public information is immediately incorporated into share prices. In truth most markets are not efficient and thus it is possible for an informed decision-maker to beat them. Even if supermarket queues were efficient, no queue would be a superior bet, because expert supermarket customers would quickly join any queue that was likely to be quicker.

More likely, queues are not efficient because few have much to gain from becoming expert queuers. Some have other considerations, such as minimising the distance walked, while others shop rarely, so the calculations are more trouble than they are worth.

And unlike the stock market, which a financial wizard can make more efficient by outweighing the foolish decisions of small traders, in the supermarket a single expert queuer has a limited effect on the distribution of queuing times.

I can advise you to steer clear of elderly ladies with vouchers, but more advice would be self-defeating. Too many of your rivals would read it.

Yours, from the express checkout, The Undercover Economist

Dear Undercover Economist,

I find it so convenient to talk on my mobile phone while driving. Must I really stop?

– Erica Talbot

Dear Ms Talbot,

Since your petulant tone suggests that you believe that the law should not apply to you, let us consider the issue independently of the legal position.

Talking on your mobile while driving makes you more than four times more likely to have an accident. While three thousand people die each year on British roads, mobile phones are responsible for about 2 per cent of these fatalities – roughly sixty deaths last year.

We continue to allow driving because it has its benefits.

Talking and driving conceivably also has benefits. Clearly a more considered view is required to weigh those benefits against the grim costs.

The AEI-Brookings Joint Center for Regulatory Studies, an American think-tank, often publishes such analysis. Its paper on this subject estimated that the cost of talking while driving – in terms of damage, injury and death – was about fifteen dollars for each American citizen. Yet the paper estimates that the average citizen is willing to pay about sixty-five dollars to keep making calls while driving (this estimate comes, in part, from looking at mobile-phone bills).

All this suggests that there are cheaper ways to save lives than with an outright ban – such as taxing garrulous drivers and using the money to pay for ambulances.

As for your personal decisions, using a hands-free device and postponing trivial calls would save lives for a small cost.

Overall you simply have to decide whether you are happy to enjoy benefits for yourself despite the costs you inflict on others. It may be economically efficient but it is still selfish and rude.

Yours, hands-free, The Undercover Economist

Dear Undercover Economist,

I am a close confidant of one of Nigeria's most powerful families. The wife of a former top government official who served in the previous military regime in Nigeria, and is currently having a face-off with the authorities, wishes to move out of Africa the sum of US$15m. It is my client's desire that this deal be handled as quietly as possible. If you agree to receive this fund on behalf of my client, please supply me with your bank account

details and I shall arrange for the release of this sum of
US$15m to you. Your commission shall be a down
payment of 15 per cent of the total sum. And annual 5
per cent of the after-tax returns on investment you are to
manage for the first five years.

God bless. As I await your response.

– Bernard Nwazojie

Dear Mr Nwazojie,

You are on the verge of making a serious mistake. You are offering me two million dollars up-front, plus a few hundred thousand a year for five years. In exchange all you require of me is my bank details. These terms seem highly generous. There are about fifty million people in this country with bank accounts. One of the others might be willing to work with you for substantially less than you have offered me. You should really shop around a bit.

Indeed both non cooperative and cooperative game theoretic models suggest that, as there are so many account holders, but only one fifteen milion dollars looking for a home, your bargaining power is almost limitless. You could hold an online auction to find out who was willing to receive the cash for the smallest cut; but at least solicit a few competitive bids. Otherwise for me to take your money would feel like fraud.

God bless, The Undercover Economist

Halloween is not far off and I dread the rapping of little knuckles on my door. The implicit bargain is pretty clear: if I refuse to provide bags of sweets, I can expect to have dog mess posted through my letterbox or some similar fate. How should I respond to this blackmail?

– Victor Harrington, Surrey

Dear Victor,

Strictly speaking, it's extortion not blackmail. But that's not the largest flaw in your analysis. Your error is in failing to appreciate that the so-called 'bargain' you describe is dependent on threats that are not credible.

You need to start by thinking about the final stage of the game, when the local brats decide whether to victimise you or not. If they're vicious enough to go through the considerable trouble of collecting dog excrement, they will do that whether or not you've paid up. It is more likely that they won't bother. Either way your prior action does not impinge on their strategy space or their pay-offs. In other words it doesn't make any difference whether you give them sweets. It is more sensible for them to spread rumours of dire fates awaiting tight-fisted neighbours than it is actually to do anything to make the rumours come true.

The analysis would change, of course, if children were able to build up a reputation for credible threats and promises. You would know that giving sweets would make you safe, but otherwise punishment would be certain.

For many threats and promises it is crucial to take these

reputation-building effects into account if you wish to understand what will happen. However, in the case of your local scamps, reputation-building might be a little easier if they were not all wearing interchangeable Halloween masks.

Yours bravely, The Undercover Economist

Dear Undercover Economist,

I take a daily commuter train to London, which is standing room only from my station. I am ready to offer cash to anyone prepared to give up their seat. How should I conduct proceedings to obtain the best price and would a season ticket-style arrangement be possible with any regular fellow passenger from up the line?

– Daniel Confino, London

Dear Mr Confino,

You should organise an auction for a seat, seeking the commuter who will relinquish his or her place for the lowest fee. So far, so obvious. But there is more to be said.

First, the transaction costs of a spot-market transaction are large. You would have to wander up and down a crowded train soliciting bids. I predict that you would be arrested, or worse. Therefore your idea of procuring a quiet long-term deal in advance is very wise. Simply post notices in stations inviting bids via email.

Because you are securing an unusual asset in unusual circumstances, bidders will find it hard to collude or to form sensible views as to how much they should be compensated in order to stand for an hour every morning. It is highly likely that at least one bidder will be foolishly optimistic and offer to sell for a laughably low price – the notorious 'winner's curse'.

But don't be too smug. Winners who feel cursed have a habit of reneging. You should draw up a clear contract, specifying the permitted number of days off and the penalties for default. Don't pay in advance and make sure you secure a performance bond to be posted with a neutral third party.

These precautions will put off some people – but it is better to do business on sustainable terms than to create a dissatisfied person on the other side of the deal. Especially since you have no idea what they may decide to smear on your seat.

Yours, reclining, The Undercover Economist

Dear Undercover Economist,

I have a long-running argument with my husband. He always reverses into parking spaces. I prefer to drive in forwards and reverse out. Who is correct?

– Maddie French, Cirencester

Dear Maddie,

Your question takes us into deep waters. Start by observing that it is, presumably, easier to drive forward than to reverse. Your husband is therefore delaying gratification while you are delaying difficulties. Mainstream economic theory is perfectly clear on this point: your husband is being silly. It is pain, not pleasure, which should be delayed, if for no other reason than we are all mortal.

But our analysis must go further than this. If you park for an hour, even a slight difference in ease of reversing in versus reversing out should swamp any benefits from delaying the difficulty. For example, if it is just one-tenth of one per cent harder to reverse out than to reverse in, then you should reverse in. If you preferred to delay the pain by an hour, bear in mind that one-tenth of one per cent per hour compounds to a substantial annual interest rate: around one-third of a million per cent. To drive in forwards and reverse out would show either impatience verging on insanity or a staggering incapacity to predict the near future.

There is another consideration: you are trading off reversing under conditions of certainty versus reversing under conditions of uncertainty. You do not know what the car park may look like in an hour, whether it will be crowded or whether you will be in a hurry. Having to reverse out under adverse circumstances is a low-risk but high-impact event. My advice is position yourself ready to leave at a moment's notice: the car park at Safeway can be an unpredictable place.

Yours, prepared for a quick getaway, The Undercover Economist

----

I am worried about the damage we wreak on our planet and I want to do my bit to reduce my personal environmental impact. I was thinking of moving to the country and living a more self-sufficient life. But is there a better way?

– Jocelyn Hathaway, London

Dear Jocelyn,

You should ask yourself, rather, if there is a worse way. London may not appear to be the model of sustainable development but it is an organic commune compared with what would happen if the other seven million inhabitants selfishly decided to move to the country.

Tightly packed, rich cities such as London are easily the most environmentally friendly way to enjoy modern life. Wealthy people squeeze into cosy apartments. Cocktail bars and sharp suits are green ways to spend cash compared with maintaining an extensive garden saturated with fertilisers and pesticides.

Denser cities mean more efficient transport. Compare the commuting patterns of London with the sprawling city of Atlanta. Even before the congestion charge, only 10 per cent of commutes into central London took place in cars. In Atlanta 90 per cent of commutes were in cars, three-quarters with the driver unaccompanied.

Manhattan, the densest and richest city of all, was recently described in the *New Yorker* as 'a utopian environmentalist community' and is vastly more energy-efficient, per person, than any of the fifty American states.

All this without requiring anyone to eat lentils or live like a pauper.

My advice to you is to forget all this self-centred nonsense about moving to the country. Instead put double-glazing in your flat, travel to work by bike and relax in the smug knowledge that you are living in one of the greenest cities on the planet.

Yours environmentally, The Undercover Economist

Dear Undercover Economist,

I am a regular reader but have found some of your recent choices a bit weak. If you are suffering a dearth of interesting questions, the price of bribing you to publish something boring should currently be falling. What is your current price?

– Paul Palley, by email

Dear Mr Palley,

Your observation is so charming that I decided to publish it for nothing. If only your letter contained any insight, I would be tempted to bribe you to send more. Sadly it does not.

In the absence of bribes I would select only the most stimulating readers' contributions, so bribery should push the quality of published contributions down, not up. If you have found recent letters insipid, perhaps the explanation is that they came packaged with offers I found difficult to refuse.

You must also remember that the price of bribing me would rise if space in the *Financial Times* was more limited. That's easy to arrange: it is in my interests to invent fictional letters to generate artificial scarcity and drive up prices.

But your analysis contains still deeper flaws. It is actually very difficult for me to take a decent-sized bribe. Economists realise that corruption in public life is not just a matter of criminal temperament but of opportunity. The economist Robert Klitgaard famously proposed a formula for bribery: corruption equals monopoly, plus discretion, minus accountability.

Klitgaard's formula clearly predicts that my actions in writing the 'Dear Economist' column are squeaky clean. Admittedly I have the discretion to choose dull letters if bribed to do so. But my monopoly power is severely limited: the *FT*'s editors would sell their own grandmothers so if a tempting bribe was ever offered, you can be sure they would undercut me.

Yours incorruptibly, The Undercover Economist

Dear Undercover Economist,

My girlfriend and I have diametrically opposed views on the ethics of dwarf-tossing – the sport where very large men compete to see who can throw a very small man the furthest. She says that the tossed are forced into it because of their limited employment options, like prostitutes. I think these men have made a conscious, free decision to do what they do and are compensated for it. Can we get a referee's call?

– J. Cheng, Stanford, California

Dear Mr Cheng,

I recognise the parallel between a 'tossee' and a prostitute, but hardly imagine that this resolves your argument. As for being 'forced' into the job by limited options, I imagine this is true in the sense that both prostitutes and tossees would prefer to be movie stars, given the choice. So what?

Yet you may find another comparison instructive. Think of workers in developing-world sweatshops, struggling to make cheap products for our enjoyment. In all three cases the situation is discomfiting to the sensitive observer. In all three cases we should respect those doing these horrible jobs enough to see that they are likely to be choosing the best of the alternatives available. Banning sweatshop labour or prostitution is an ethical luxury that can, and does, damage the interests of the supposed victims. (I cannot speak with authority about bans on dwarf-tossing.)

But I am disturbed by the equanimity with which you seem to view dwarf-tossing. The right response is to improve the alternatives. Sweatshops tend to produce their own alternatives as productivity and education grow. It is not clear how dwarf-tossing contributes to better alternatives for very small men; perhaps you and your girlfriend could abandon your squabbling in favour of finding some practical solution?

Yours ethically, The Undercover Economist

Dear Undercover Economist,

Our local council does not collect cardboard and plastics for recycling, presumably for economic reasons. Yet in our household we have felt it our moral duty to separate those items and deliver them each weekend to our local recycling centre for processing. If a centralised collection system is unworkable, does that mean our individual effort is detrimental to the global environment?

– Ju-Yen Tan, West London

Dear Ju-Yen,

Governments do many things that are economically wasteful and neglect to do others that would be economically efficient. So I wouldn't take your local council's behaviour as a guide to your own.

In fact recycling can sometimes be financially viable even before considering the environmental benefits: companies have been profitably recycling office paper, aluminium and steel for more than twenty years. But such recycling programmes enjoy economies of scale that you do not.

As for sorting and delivering the rubbish yourself, the sad – or perhaps relieving – fact is that the case for home recycling is tenuous. It would be all very well if you walked past the plastics bank on your way to the tube station every morning, but if you are making an additional car journey to the recycling centre you are using energy, causing congestion and consuming scarce fossil fuels. The net environmental benefits of your trip are small and may even be negative.

The economic benefits are lower. The most significant cost is the value of your time. Do not underestimate this. If you get a kick out of sorting through your rubbish, don't let me stop you, but this has not traditionally been seen as an inspiring task. Don't forget that the price of most commodities has been falling for decades, if not centuries, with one clear exception: the price of labour.

Please dispose of my answer responsibly, The Undercover Economist

Dear Undercover Economist,

'Pascal's wager' states that even if it is unlikely that God exists, it is rational to believe in his existence since disbelief risks infinite unhappiness for eternity.

But even if hell exists, its torments are likely to be so intense as to have a high discount rate. Although any individual moment in hell might be infinitely painful, the sheer intensity should lower the expectation that such pain might continue through eternity. Multiply that by the low probability of the existence of a deity that actually operates as hypothesised and the future expected value of both heavenly bliss and hellish torment should converge close to zero. Doesn't Epicurus make more sense than Pascal?

– Karthik Sankaran, New York

Dear Karthik,

Infinity doesn't work like that. Pascal's wager does not depend on the eternal duration of reward and punishment. A moment in heaven is infinitely pleasurable so even if heaven lasts no longer than that, that moment outweighs a lifetime of Epicurean pleasures.

Even if you believe the probability that God exists is tiny, a tiny chance of a moment of infinite bliss outweighs a lifetime of large but finite bliss.

Perhaps you think that Pascal's wager displays flawed logic. But wait. The economist Alex Tabarrok points out that if there is even a tiny chance that Pascal is right, a tiny chance of a tiny chance of a second of infinite bliss is still infinitely valuable.

Now if you give me all your money, I'll intercede with God

on your behalf and increase your chance of going to heaven. Of course there is only a tiny chance that my intercession will help, but a tiny chance of infinite bliss is, again, infinitely valuable.

Please send your cheque via the *FT*, and quickly please – I've already given Professor Tabarrok all my cash.

Yours ecclesiastically, The Undercover Economist

Dear Undercover Economist,

I have a drawer full of odd socks. Where do the missing socks go?

– Christian Turner, Washington, DC

Dear Mr Turner,

Like most investments in physical capital, your sock supply is depreciating. Depreciation happens. I suggest that you should work out how to minimise the damage, rather than questing after the lost socks.

The problem is simple: each half of a unique pair of socks is a perfect complement to the other half. The marginal value of the first sock is close to zero, unless you favour unconventional dress. The marginal value of the second sock is a matching pair of socks. The result of a lost sock is in fact the loss of two socks.

This problem also plagues machines: when one component

fails, the entire machine may need to be scrapped. The solution is to make interchangeable parts so that the damaged piece can be replaced. Interchangeability dates back at least to Gutenberg and the printing press in the 1450s, but formidable technical problems meant that interchangeability didn't become common until the assembly lines of the early twentieth century. Generations of engineers knew that the struggle across the centuries would eventually pay economic dividends. You, on the other hand, do not need to wait for some hard-won technological breakthrough. You should have no difficulty providing interchangeable parts for your sock drawer. Throw out your pre-industrial inventory, then go out and buy two dozen pairs of identical socks at once.

I personally find this method works extremely well. What you lose in sartorial flexibility you make up in a less wasteful pattern of sock depreciation, and a vastly quicker search of the sock drawer each morning. Your socks will still vanish mysteriously but you are far less likely to ask metaphysical questions about the phenomenon.

Yours, well-matched, The Undercover Economist

———————

Dear Undercover Economist,

My dentist tells me that I should floss but what do you think?

– William Henderson, Virginia

Dear William,

You may be misremembering John Maynard Keynes's famous wish that economists should aspire to be thought of 'as humble, competent people on a level with dentists'.

I don't think Keynes ever believed that economists should become dentists. Fortunately for you, Bryan Caplan, an economist at George Mason University, thinks otherwise.

Professor Caplan's dentist, like yours, is quick to list the benefits of flossing in rather vague terms. No doubt the benefits are real. But are they greater than the costs? Flossing is tedious, uncomfortable and undignified. You can quantify the costs of a lifetime of flossing for yourself: I suggest that you ask your dentist to quantify the benefits before you make a decision.

Professor Caplan's dentist didn't seem to understand the question so Caplan turned to the scientific journal *Nature* for enlightenment.

It turns out that dentistry itself may not be as useful as Keynes believed: regular dental check-ups are likely to give you no more than five extra teeth when you're seventy-five – assuming you live that long. This is a modest and distant reward for a lifetime of being drilled.

Of course this column shouldn't be mistaken for informed medical advice. Neither Caplan nor I know a thing about dentistry. But I believe that if economists make a bit of an effort to understand dental health and hygiene, then dentists should meet us halfway and produce that cost-benefit analysis.

You may think this is missing the point: flossing also helps to produce more kissable breath. Perhaps most economists feel that bad breath is the least of our worries.

Kissably yours, The Undercover Economist

Dear Undercover Economist,

Governments like to promote innovation. But ever greater innovation means ever greater use of resources, disposability of goods, consumer spending and (one surmises) social envy. Is there a case for suppressing innovation?

– Marion Hancock, by email

Dear Marion,

There are two ways to raise purchasing power: investment or innovation. Investment means buying big machines so that each worker operates more equipment. It is hard to see how this is more environmentally friendly than innovation. It is also self-limiting: all the investment budget goes on replacing worn-out machines.

By contrast innovative ideas consume no resources at all. They are particularly useful when there are many people on the planet because everyone can benefit from a piece of software, a better design for the mousetrap or the theory of germs. Not everyone can benefit from my electric hand drill.

Nor do innovative products use more resources. Today's expensive consumer products are tiny, or do not physically exist at all – for example the four thousand issues of the *New Yorker* that my wife gave me for Christmas are stored digitally.

It is true that if I was poor enough then I would have received no magazines, digital or otherwise. So perhaps you are not really in favour of suppressing innovation but of ending economic growth entirely. This has proved possible – for example, in Mao's China or the dying days of the Soviet Union. Environmental Eden did not result.

At least an end to innovation might (you surmise) return us to the envy-free days when my great-grandmother might have been your great-grandfather's scullery maid.

But I don't wish to find out.

Innovatively yours, The Undercover Economist

Dear Undercover Economist,

Is there an economic law to explain why tradesmen always arrive after or toward the end of the time slot they give a customer. If they advise 'between nine and twelve', they will never come at 9 a.m. and usually won't arrive until 1 p.m.

– Andy Moffat, London

Dear Andy,

I might have to request more data in support of your theory before I swallow it. Having just moved house, I've had four separate appointments with tradesmen or deliveries in the past two days. All came less than an hour after the start of their time slot and one was slightly early. We tend to forget these happy occasions and recall our disappointments instead.

But I don't want to dismiss your theory entirely. Even allowing for our natural tendency to recall the most egregious tardiness, I agree that tradesmen often miss their promised slot. The reason is simple: they have little incentive to keep their promises.

Most of your interactions with tradesmen are one-shot affairs.

You've never seen them before, you'll never see them again and quite likely you picked them at random out of a business directory because your living-room ceiling just collapsed. If their business largely depends on strangers like you, why would they inconvenience themselves to build up a reputation? The few tradesmen with whom you deal frequently are more likely to be punctual.

If you want to solve the problem, the necessary incentive structure is quite simple. Call your man at 9 a.m. and tell him he'll get an extra twenty quid if he stops the job he's doing and comes over immediately. If enough other people are doing this, that may explain why you always have to wait until after lunch.

Unreliably yours, The Undercover Economist

Dear Undercover Economist,

Is it worth bothering to pay for municipal car parking? I only get caught out every now and then, and it's such a bother finding change for the meter compared with writing the occasional cheque.

– Hilary Potts, Ealing

Dear Hilary,

A similar question once occurred to Gary Becker, then a professor at Columbia University. Running late to a viva examination of a doctoral student, he drove to the university and then quickly weighed the cost of paying for parking against the chance of being fined. He then asked the unfortunate student to discuss the optimal behaviour of the authorities who set the charges and penalties. The story ends happily: the student passed, Becker avoided a ticket and won the Nobel Prize.

If it is true, as you imply, that the expected cost of risking a ticket is lower than the expected cost of paying up front, then your municipal authorities are giving you a surprisingly easy decision. It is obvious that you should not pay – or more precisely that you should pay large sums occasionally rather than small sums every time.

Many people would find this strategy made for anxious shopping trips but you seem to have nerves of steel. This is rational: unless the fines are very large, or your income much lower than that of most people who find small sums of money irritating, the unpredictability of parking fines should not itself seriously lower your utility.

Nor do I see any moral objection to your actions. As long as you park only in legitimate spaces and pay your parking fines promptly, you seem to be abiding by the rules of the game, even if your opening gambit within those rules is unorthodox. Your only concern should be wheel clamps.

Rationally yours, The Undercover Economist

Dear Undercover Economist,

I live in Bondi Junction, Sydney, about seventy metres above sea level. On sunny mornings I cycle down to Bondi Beach for a swim before work. Coasting three kilometres downhill is fun but puffing back up is tedious. Like many people, I prefer to save up the best for last. Is there some way I can store up the downhill utility and draw on it as I pedal uphill? An analogy might be Kentucky Fried Chicken: I am an occasional consumer, and I love the taste as it goes down, but hate the queasy feeling afterwards. I'm sure I would eat more KFC if I could get the queasy feeling over with first and then enjoy the taste. There must be loads of demand out there for a delayed-utility function.

– Alex Dobes, Sydney

Dear Alex,

It is fascinating to hear that you would chomp down more fried food if only the experience could begin with feeling sick. Sadly I know of nothing that can delay utility until the appropriate moment, with the possible exception of chocolate. But I can suggest the next best thing: since your quest for delayed gratification is so extreme, you simply need to save all the money you can and spend it in your twilight years. Money cannot directly buy utility but it helps.

I would be happy to take all the money you can spare – which should be most of it – and give it back to you at a later date. The later you want it, the less I will give back but, apparently, the more this will be worth to you.

I am already licking my lips in anticipation.

Yours, in due course, The Undercover Economist

Dear Undercover Economist,

I have read in the pages of the *FT* that copper prices in 2006 were so high that copper coins were worth more as copper than as coins. Should I have been breaking open the savings jar and melting down its contents?

– Morris Kelvin, Aberdeen

Dear Mr Kelvin,

It is perfectly true that the price of copper not so long ago was so high that the face value of a tonne of copper coins was less than the price of a tonne of copper. You may have read this in the *FT* and erroneously concluded that coins were worth more as copper. In fact the price of copper would have to move substantially higher before you consider melting your loose change.

What you have forgotten is that the price of copper can fall as well as rise. A piece of copper worth 1.1 pence may be worth 1.3 pence tomorrow, or 0.9 pence. A copper penny worth 1.1 pence as scrap may be worth 1.3 pence tomorrow but will never be worth less than a penny. When copper prices are very volatile – and in 2006 they were – your best strategy is to hold on to the penny as a penny. You can cash in if prices rise still further, while knowing that a collapse on copper prices will not destroy the value of your penny.

If the penny becomes worth five pence as scrap, then the price floor of a penny becomes almost irrelevant, and you can melt and sell.

That said, I could not advise you exactly when to cash in: that would depend not only on the price of copper but on how much that price is bouncing around. Financial wizards exist who profess to be able to calculate such things but I suspect they would charge you rather more than pocket change.

Yours, coining it, The Undercover Economist

Dear Undercover Economist,

It was my birthday recently and I made some resolutions: to slim for the beach, read more serious novels, save money and quit smoking. I am doing OK on the cigarettes so far but I am already back to watching *Big Brother* and I have put on three pounds. Did I take on too much at once?

– Rebecca Furniss, Parsons Green, London

Dear Rebecca,

An interesting new paper by three University of Michigan economists argues that willpower is a scarce resource like any other. You cannot exceed your allocation of willpower any more than you can buy a round of drinks with an empty purse.

It's a plausible view: economic psychologists have found that people make more impulsive decisions if they have already had to resist earlier temptations than if they come fresh to the chocolate bar. Many of us have caved in and given ourselves a 'reward' after a day of hard work.

It seems likely that your success in kicking the smoking habit has drained you of the psychic resources to read anything other than Dan Brown. Worse, were you to redouble your efforts to plough through something by James Joyce, your cigarette habit might return, leaving you at risk of becoming the most cultured corpse in the morgue.

The solution is clear enough. First, outsource tough decisions whenever you can. Set up an automatic savings plan and cut up your credit card so you will not have to resist the temptation to spend too much money. Buy food online so that you do not have to walk past the Ben and Jerry's and use up your valuable powers of self-denial.

And if you ever feel like reaching for the cigarettes again, top up your willpower by reaching instead for the freezer and the remote control.

Temptedly yours, The Undercover Economist

Dear Undercover Economist,

I notice that your book, *The Undercover Economist*, has a list price of £17.99. In it you emphasise that rationality and calculation underlie economic behaviour. If so why do so many prices end in .99? Do consumers really think that £17.99 is only £17?

– Daniella Acker, via email

Dear Daniella,

A more likely explanation – from Steven Landsburg, an economist at the University of Rochester – is that these prices are designed not to exploit incompetence but to fight dishonesty.

A typical bookshop will experience a certain amount of shop-lifting, especially of products as tempting as my book. Nobody is better placed to benefit from shoplifting than the shop assistants.

If books – or any products – were roundly priced at £10, £15 or £20, then customers would frequently offer the correct change. In such cases it would be simple for the shop assistant to bag the item without ringing it through the till and to pocket the cash.

The book would appear to have been stolen by the customer but this is a far more attractive proposition than trying to fence a stolen copy of *A la recherche du temps perdu*, or even *The Undercover Economist*, and the risk is probably lower. All rational shoplifters should get jobs in shops.

However, the more awkward the pricing, the more unlikely those thieving till-jockeys are to be able to pull off the trick. The customer will want change and is likely to challenge a shop assistant who reaches into his pocket to make it.

If this theory is true then we should not expect to see those 99p endings in shops manned by their owners, nor at internet shops where shoplifting is impossible.

I note that the price of my book on Amazon ends not in .99 but .78.

Your crimebusting friend, The Undercover Economist

––––––––––

Dear Undercover Economist,

How would an economist respond to the phrase 'money is the root of all evil'?

– Mike Choe, via email

Dear Mike,

Economists always seem to talk in pounds and pence, yet few economic models contain any reference to the stuff.

The reason why economists will use strange phrases such as 'the value of a kiss is forty-nine pounds' is not that they think money is particularly important but simply that it is a convenient way to measure things. If a toffee apple is worth seven pounds then a kiss is as good as seven toffee apples; however, if the toffee apples cost six pounds and the kiss costs fifty pounds then the toffee apples are a better buy.

All that said, why do we have money at all, rather than using – for instance – toffee apples as a medium of exchange? One reason is that the price of toffee apples may fluctuate wildly, which means that although I could in principle write a contract denominated in toffee apples, it would be hard to have much confidence in what that contract really meant. Contracts in the ancient world were sometimes denominated in salt because it had a stable price. These days pounds are even better.

A complementary explanation is that money is a simple way for people to gain credibility. I can settle my debts by writing a note that says 'I owe you one kiss', but I may not make good that promise, nor will you be able to use my IOU to pay for anything else. If instead I give you forty-nine pounds, this is a promise made by the UK Treasury, a more dependable debtor.

In short we need money because people simply don't trust each other. In the words of economists Nobuhiro Kiyotaki and John Moore, 'Evil is the root of all money.'

Yours, for a price, The Undercover Economist

Dear Undercover Economist,

I have the habit of setting my watch five minutes fast. This fools me into avoiding being three minutes late for meetings or the train – well, more often than not – and instead being two minutes early. But if I am a rational economic agent, how do I succeed in fooling myself so systematically?

– Mark, Oxford

Dear Mark,

That is a big 'if'. Economists frequently explain eccentric behaviour with a model of two rational agents in one body, battling to outwit each other.

In your case one agent (the one who is always late) is impatient: the risk of missing a train in half an hour is unimportant compared with the instant satisfaction to be derived from having one more sip of coffee. Your more patient half disagrees. There seems to be some sort of stickiness in your perception of time. Stickiness is a feature of retail prices because retailers will absorb a certain amount of inflation before spending money on repainting signs and reprinting catalogues. However, at some stage – perhaps a 5 or 10 per cent increase in the price level – the fixed cost of that reprinting must be paid.

Your impatient self clearly suffers from a similar fixed cost of carrying out subtraction. If your watch was, say, forty-seven minutes fast, this fixed cost would have to be borne every time you looked at it, because being forty-seven minutes early for everything is even more costly than having to perform mental arithmetic. Five minutes, like a 1 per cent increase in the price level, is more tolerable.

To summarise: you have a split personality, a warped view of time and are too lazy to do simple sums. Now put down this reply: I suspect you are running late for something.

Yours punctually, The Undercover Economist

Dear Undercover Economist,

I have a question for you. You have a piece of bread and you are full enough to give it to someone else. In front of you, ten guys are waiting for your charity. You can say only one sentence to them.

But with only this one sentence, you need to find out who is the most hungry guy. What are you going to say?

– Myeong Hyeon, via email

Dear Myeong Hyeon,

This is an interesting poser, although in fact I would run a mile if confronted by ten hungry guys clamouring for my focaccia. That is, perhaps, quibbling, but my main complaint about your question is more serious.

Perhaps you believe that there is little difference between economics and the parlour games of logicians, but in this particular case there is all the difference in the world.

A basic proposition of economics is that talk is cheap. Nothing these worthy fellows could say conveys any information to me. A crook can tell the same sob story as the most desperate beggar.

One possibility, then, is that I could carry out intrusive background checks on these characters. However, that is expensive and tiresome for all concerned – and since the largest providers of pieces of bread are governments, there are concerns over abuses of information, too.

Alternatively, and more elegantly, I could hand over bread only to those people who give me a signal that a well-fed con man would not be willing to give. For example I could demand that the recipient of the bread first wallow in a muddy puddle. But this, like many signals, is wasteful. Better if the signal was also socially productive so that I could hand out bread in exchange for useful work. We call this arrangement 'getting a job'.

Yours uncharitably, The Undercover Economist

Dear Undercover Economist,

Why should I wash my car? It will be dirty again tomorrow!

– Chris Smith, Hampshire

Dear Chris,

Why indeed should you brush your teeth? They too will be dirty tomorrow. Such arguments may impress a certain melancholy breed of philosopher, but economics offers clear advice. You cannot keep your car exactly as clean as you would want so must balance the costs of washing it against the costs of having it too dirty.

Consider an analogous problem: how much money to keep in

211

your wallet? Too much and you will suffer from theft or inflation. Too little and the wallet serves no purpose. Since it is troublesome to obtain cash, the rational customer will take out more than is ideal, gradually spend the money until there is less than ideal, and then replenish the wallet.

A graph of cash held over time would look like a sawtooth, regularly leaping up and sloping down. Now that we have ATMs it is easier to get cash, we do so more often, hold cash balances closer to the optimum, and the saw is finely grained.

The sawtooth model applies more widely. It explains, for example, why you should – as many people do – cut your hair too short so that as it grows it is on average the correct length.

As for your car, you must find a way to wash it so that it is cleaner than you would ideally like, which considering your question should not be difficult. Consider a full service wash with wax and carpet shampooing. The car will be so extravagantly, embarrassingly clean that for a week or two after the wash you will be waiting impatiently for the dirt to begin accumulating.

Spotlessly yours, The Undercover Economist

Dear Undercover Economist,

I like the idea of smoking; people who do it seem to get a lot of pleasure from it. But I don't want it seriously to curtail my longevity. So at what age could I sensibly start smoking in order to achieve sufficient pleasure to make the shortening of lifespan worthwhile?

– Peter, London

212

Dear Peter,

You're right to point out that smoking has benefits as well as costs, and that implies that it might be perfectly rational to smoke. You also implicitly accept that smoking is addictive since your cigarette consumption plan seems to be to start and never stop. But this consumption plan may be poorly timed. For one thing there is some evidence that if you smoke while young and can quit before you die of a heart attack, your risk of heart disease rapidly recedes. (Don't ask me about the cancer risk, though. I'm an economist, not an epidemiologist.)

Leaving aside the medical questions, there's the social side. If you're twenty years old and smoke in full defiance of the risks, you still have a chance to look brash, daring and just a little bit sexy. If people see you smoking at sixty, they won't realise your brilliance in taking up the habit at age fifty-eight. They'll simply assume that, pathetically, you've never been able to quit.

My advice, then, is that the optimal consumption path for cigarettes is either never to start or to start young and stop fairly quickly. Which you choose depends on, among other things, your estimate of your own willpower. This is hard to guess in advance. Perhaps you should tell your doctor you plan to start smoking and ask him for advice about how to quit once you've started. At least you'll get his attention.

Addictively yours, The Undercover Economist

Dear Undercover Economist,

I am an immigrant who has lived in England long
enough to know that I should never leave home without
an umbrella. Many of my colleagues lack my foresight,
which means that I often find myself bumping into them
in the rain.

I always offer to share my umbrella and have noticed a
pattern. Foreigners always accept. Indeed one New
Yorker actually links her arm with mine as we walk. But
those whose families have lived here for generations
prefer getting soaked.

A cost-benefit analysis would seem to suggest my
umbrella is the better option. Yet fear of intimacy
appears to trump self-interest. Can you explain?

– Cosmo, London

Dear Cosmo,

You do not seem to hold British Londoners in high regard. You
think we are stupid, in that we repeatedly leave our umbrellas at
home despite the climate. You also believe us to be self-interested;
you are sure that we crave the umbrella that you, the clever foreigner,
has thought to carry. And you dismiss us as emotionally distant,
unlike that perky little New Yorker with whom you so enjoy
strolling in the rain.

There is an alternative to the view that we are selfish, unap-
proachable idiots. It is that we disapprove of umbrellas, viewing
them as befitting only Bulgarian assassins. What, after all, is an
umbrella but a way of redirecting rain on to other people? The
rim of spikes, too, went out with Queen Boudicca. London is a

busy place; it would simply be unsupportable if the British behaved as you do. Until recently a strong cultural norm dealt with this problem. Now that your immigrant umbrellas are causing a public nuisance, there is only one rational response: a hefty congestion charge-style tax on umbrellas.

Yours dryly, The Undercover Economist

Dear Undercover Economist,

This Christmas and New Year I expect to encounter a lot of drunks on the road. In fact I may well be one of them. Should I feel guilty? And should I be worried?

– Mr F. Jones, London

Dear Mr Jones,

It has always been difficult to test the effect of alcohol on drivers let loose on the roads. The difficulty is this: if half of all crashes involve drunks, that may be because drinking impairs your driving or it may be because there are a lot of drunks on the road – and we can only guess at how many drunk drivers there are.

But the economists Steven Levitt and Jack Porter realised that it was possible to say more, by looking at how often drunk drivers crashed into each other. If 10 per cent of drivers drink, and if drunk drivers are as safe as any other kind of driver and randomly mixed among the sober drivers, then only 1 per cent of two-vehicle crashes should involve two drunks.

Drunk-on-drunk crashes are much more common than one would expect, given the number of drunk-on-sober crashes, allowing Levitt and Porter to reach firm conclusions about the risks of drink-driving.

They find a very large effect. Drivers who have been drinking are seven times more likely to cause a fatal crash; those who have drunk over the legal limit (in the US) are thirteen times more likely to cause a fatal crash. You might also bear in mind another finding from the paper: 'The great majority of alcohol-related driving fatalities occur to the drinking drivers themselves and their passengers.' That should be sobering.

Yours, The Undercover Economist

Dear Undercover Economist,

I use the same password for all my email and internet-portal accounts (online shopping, etc.). Now I am worried about losing it to an identity thief. What should I do?

– Confused Kid

Dear Confused Kid,

Rick Smith, information security expert at the University of St Thomas in Minnesota, summarises the conundrum: 'The password must be impossible to remember and never written down.' The typical password is a jumble of characters that must be changed frequently. When you type it in the computer obscures what you are typing, giving your visual memory no chance. Congratulations if you can cope with all this, let alone duplicate the feat twenty times.

There are some tricks you can rely on – for instance your passwords could be obscure acronyms inspired by song lyrics. Yet the dilemma remains: either use the same password for each account or write them down and put them under your mouse mat.

Impossible password guidelines have been developed by security professionals wishing to cover their backsides. Fine. Now you must cover yours. First, consider who picks up the pieces if things go wrong.

Your current approach is discouraged, rather than forbidden, by banks. But if you wrote down your password, security breaches would become your problem.

Second, do not be depressed. Many accounts have obvious passwords: the user's name, their partner's or simply 'password'. And up to one-third of users are thought to write them down. Fraudsters like easy targets so remember: you may not need to be smarter than them, merely smarter than the guy whose password is 'password'.

Yours securely, The Undercover Economist

Dear Undercover Economist,

I often share a taxi home with friends and wonder how best to split the bill? When dropping a friend off first, I have received contributions varying from nothing to the full fare. If I get out first, what should I pay? As a woman with a large collection of frivolous shoes, walking home is a last resort.

– Frances, Brussels

Dear Frances,

Of course contributions vary.

In a bar with friends, haven't you noticed that sometimes somebody pays for your drink and at other times you buy a round for everyone?

But in the long run the saving should be divided fairly – a word with many interpretations. If three friends would have paid €4, €8 and €12 for taxis along the same route, and now must pay €12 in total, the total saving is €12.

That saving could be divided equally, €4 apiece, meaning fares of zero, €4 and €8. Or it could be divided in proportion to the original fares, meaning fares of €2, €4 and €6. Or the first leg could be split three ways, the second leg halved, and the third leg paid by the final passenger, implying fares of €1.34, €3.34 and €7.34.

There is no magic formula.

That is why no economist would share a cab without agreeing terms beforehand.

Yours equitably, The Undercover Economist

Dear Undercover Economist,

I take small steps to reduce my carbon footprint (I walk, recycle, etc.) and attempt to influence others by spreading awareness of climate change. However, a friend recently accused me of being a hypocrite because of my contribution to carbon emissions when I fly for my holidays. I admit I do not weigh the damage done to the environment when planning my breaks and am not ready to forgo them. How do I preach green without breaching the walk-the-talk philosophy?

– An Apparent Pseudo-Treehugger

Dear Treehugger,

You are in good company. Most of the developed world's governments have been spouting about climate change, without adopting policies that have noticeably prevented the growth of carbon emissions.

But hypocrisy does not strike me as the issue here. In fact you are refreshingly honest – you say you do not know the impact of your travel and would not change if you did.

The problem, rather, is that most people are equally as ignorant and as self-centred as you. Few humans are capable of making serious sacrifices for the unborn grandchildren of total strangers, which is the basic selling point of voluntary action on climate change.

That leaves us with two alternative policies: hope that people chivvy each other into action or hope that governments swap some of their taxes on labour and capital for taxes on carbon. I am not holding my breath for either.

Environmentally yours, The Undercover Economist

Dear Undercover Economist,

I pay someone to clean my car three times a week. He usually does a good job of it. However, I often travel and as soon as I'm gone, the cleaner stops work. So I always come back to a dirty car.

I pay him even when I'm not around. Shouldn't he at least clean the car the day before he knows I will return, thus pretending to have been cleaning it regularly?

– D.T., Bahrain

Dear D.T.,

I can think of three explanations for this behaviour. Either the cleaner is too stupid to realise he should be skiving more subtly, or he thinks you are too stupid to notice, or he does not care if you notice.

If he is stupid or he thinks you are stupid – don't ask which – the solution is easy: say you've noticed that the car is dirty and ask him to clean it before you return.

If he does not care, that means he can try to get an equally good job elsewhere. Since the current job comes with frequent paid holidays, that is unlikely – unless you are being especially stingy.

I suggest sharper incentives. Tell him you'll pay him a bonus if you return to a clean car. Frankly, since you are paying him to clean an unused car incessantly, and he isn't doing it, any change is likely to be an improvement.

Yours, baffled, The Undercover Economist

Dear Undercover Economist,

Can economics help me pick out the perfect Christmas gift for my brother?

— Tim Maly, Ottawa, Canada

Dear Tim,

Your letter obliges me to disinter the influential research of the economist Joel Waldfogel on the 'deadweight loss of Christmas'. Fifteen years ago Waldfogel published an academic article demonstrating that the recipients of gifts would not generally have been willing to pay what it cost to provide the gift. A thirty-pound sweater was valued at twenty pounds, for example, creating a 'deadweight loss' of ten pounds. Siblings were not the most incompetent givers – that honour goes to aunts and uncles – but they were not especially competent either.

Waldfogel's work is often misinterpreted as suggesting that gift-giving is pointless. That is not true. He explicitly excluded the sentimental value of gifts from his calculations, and, of course, the sentimental value is part of the purpose of giving presents. That may explain why the economists Sara Solnick and David Hemenway have discovered that we prefer unsolicited presents to those we have specifically requested. It may also explain why gift vouchers are a bad idea: they have no sentimental value but still create deadweight loss, since many expire without being used or are sold at a loss on eBay – as the economist Jennifer Pate Offenberg has documented.

All this points to the optimal gift-giving strategy: you need to minimise the deadweight loss while maximising the sentimental value. This suggests buying small gifts and striving for emotional resonance. Look for something inexpensive and consider supplementing it with a letter, a photo or time spent together.

If you feel a financial transfer is necessary, slip a cheque into the envelope too. I wish you, your brother, and all the readers of this column an optimal Christmas.

Festively yours, The Undercover Economist

Dear Undercover Economist,

Here in Michigan we have a problem: the auto industry.

Thanks to foreign competition and the doubtful management of the Big Three car makers, the state's economy is in serious trouble in 2009. Should we just sell the state to the Chinese? There is a history of this in Michigan – we once traded the city of Toledo to Ohio in exchange for the upper peninsula. So perhaps it would be a good idea. I am quite excited about becoming a Chinese citizen. But what would be a good price?

– Mrs J., Michigan

Dear Mrs J.,

Make sure you don't sell yourselves cheap. According to the US Bureau of Economic Analysis, Michigan's GDP was \$382 billion in 2007. This is an attempt to measure the value added to all goods and services in Michigan, which includes anything from haircuts to assembling a car – but not, for instance, any components imported from out of state.

The figure of $382 billion is impressive. It would sneak Michigan into the top twenty-five economies in the world. Even China's GDP is less than nine times greater.

So how much would it cost to buy $382bn of productive power? No corporation adds nearly as much value; the economist Paul de Grauwe reckoned that in 2000 value added was $67 billion for Wal-Mart and $53 billion for Exxon, the two largest companies. Their market value at the time was about five times their value added.

If the same ratio applies in the case of Michigan, buying the state would cost the Chinese almost two trillion dollars. Fortunately this is roughly what China's State Administration of Foreign Exchange has to spend, a nice coincidence.

All this assumes that Michigan's residents, like Wal-Mart's employees, would be free to leave if they didn't like the new management.

Still, don't hold out too long. Even before the credit crunch hit, Michigan's GDP per head was falling in real terms. Your home state is a surprisingly valuable property but this may be the right time to sell.

Yours, with added value, The Undercover Economist

Introduction to the Second Edition

As Ben Franklin once nearly wrote, 'only two things in life can be said to be certain: problems, and the ability of economics to solve them'. That, at least, is the verdict from anguished correspondents across the world who continue to turn to economics for guidance. The following section presents a range of the questions that have poured in since the first edition of *Dear Undercover Economist* went to press – all served up accompanied by a healthy dose of cool, clear economic logic.

Stop Him Leaving You for the Nanny

Love and Dating

Dear Undercover Economist,

I'm a thirty-two-year-old American woman who moved to Italy about five years ago. My problems are twofold: first, dating. Seeing a single thirty-something is like finding a unicorn. Eliminate those who live with their mothers, are chain-smokers, or are shorter than me, and I'm in a convent. Second, I am being forced to re-earn an Italian BA, which could take a further year. I'd hate to turn down another degree but can I handle another year of pasta and enforced singledom? My current plan includes going to San Francisco upon my return, though I do have the choice of a semi-permanent job in the middle of nowhere.

Or I could stay in Italy.

– Crying in my cappuccino

Dear Crying,

You appear to be committed to staying in a country whose food, bureaucracy and dating scene do not suit you. Your judgement has been clouded by the sunk cost fallacy: you hoped to get another degree, great food and an Italian paramour. Things didn't work out and you have wasted five years. You're only human if you want to waste another year, but you're making a mistake. Go home.

As for your career, forget cash: a happy relationship and secure job are far more important. San Francisco is not famed for its excess of single straight men, but the demographics of

the middle of nowhere are excellent, with many eligible
bachelors.

> *Telling it to you straight,*
> *The Undercover Economist*

Dear Undercover Economist,

I have been divorced since 2007 and decided to start
dating three months ago. I recently met an artist whom I
find extremely hot! I am curious to know how much
information about myself I should divulge to him. I have
made some bad decisions in my forty-two years. I am
stable now but fear some of these things may affect his
view of me. What would be the benefit of opening up to
him before we hit a home run?

– Seeking

Dear Seeking,

It seems to me that this is all about switching costs, a concept
formalised by Paul Klemperer, an economist at Oxford
University. If breaking off this relationship will be painful
for you but easy for him, you had best get the skeletons out of
the closet immediately and hope he doesn't run a mile. It
would be worse to have loved and lost than never to have loved
at all.

If, on the other hand, your own switching costs are low, there is every reason to keep your mouth shut. Enjoy a few 'home runs', and if he later discovers that you are a former prostitute, a recovering alcoholic or a fan of Boyzone, at least you had your fun while you could.

The case for discretion is even stronger if your new beau has his own switching costs. In this case, once he has committed to the relationship he may find himself stuck with you even if he later learns the stark truth. Keep your secrets to yourself, give him a taste of what's on offer, and wait until he's hooked.

Your friendly dealer of good advice,
The Undercover Economist

Dear Undercover Economist,

Now that we have completed our family, my wife wants me to have a vasectomy, strongly hinting that she will withdraw all sexual favours unless I comply. For a long time now, the amount of sex we have been having (about once a month) has been less than I would like (a couple of times a week). While I am not an economist, I have read that positive incentives are important. Wouldn't my wife would have more chance of persuading me to have the snip if she promised me more frequent sex rather than threatening to withdraw it altogether?

– Dave, London

Dear Dave,

In traditional economics there is no important motivational difference between stick and carrot, and so I can hardly accuse your wife of bad economics in that respect.

But, even if your proposal is accepted, you face a serious problem. Your vasectomy is a one-off operation, for which you seek an ongoing future incentive. How can you be sure that your wife will stick to the deal? Economists call this the 'hold-up problem'.

You are hoping for an extra ninety bouts of intimacy per year. Since I give your marriage five more years, tops, this adds up to an extra 450 sexual encounters in total. But there is no guarantee that, after you have your operation, you will experience any of them.

The obvious answer is a performance bond. Your wife could deposit, say, £45,000 with a lawyer. Whenever the two of you contact the lawyer to confirm that intercourse has occurred, he will release £100 to your wife.

Perhaps that seems unromantic, so I have a better idea – simply secure payment in kind up front. If the two of you get busy, you should get through 450 love-making sessions within a year, perhaps sooner. You might even find you enjoy it so much that this troubled marriage perks up. I suggest you get started at once.

Yours in safety,
The Undercover Economist

Dear Undercover Economist,

My partner and I have well-defined boundaries to our relationship; they are already liberal, and we are now considering permitting liaisons with others. The benefits for my partner are enormous, as she is an attractive young woman interested in men and women alike.

I, on the other hand, am an awkward wallflower of unremarkable appearance, who has trouble attracting women. Or at least I was until I met my partner. In the years we've been together, I've received a startling amount of unsolicited attention from women who would not have looked at me twice when I was single.

Can economics explain why I'm unappealing as a singleton, but hot property when with a stunning girlfriend? More importantly, will I still be hot property in a non-monogamous setup? As a consumer I seem to be able to have my cake and eat it, but as a commodity, can I both be had and eaten?

– Confused, Paradise

Dear Confused,

Your sudden attractiveness does indeed have an economic explanation: your new admirers are rationally inferring information about you from the behaviour of your partner. She is vivacious, beautiful and intelligent, and yet she dates you; ergo you have hidden assets.

I am not sure an open relationship is wise. You are right to point out that your partner has much to gain from such an arrangement. Onlookers would rightly conclude that her commitment to you has few downsides for her, so doesn't convey much of a signal that you are a hidden gem. There is another risk. Through her experiments, your partner may discover an alternative lover who insists on a monogamous relationship. Monogamy may be a price worth paying, given that she is currently dating 'an awkward wallflower of unremarkable appearance'. You currently live in paradise; don't risk being cast out.

Yours poetically,
The Undercover Economist

Dear Undercover Economist,

I have a great boyfriend. We've been together for five years, have a son and are planning more kids. I have a good job which I would like to continue doing and that pays OK. My boyfriend earns a lot more money than me and we have a very comfortable lifestyle. We are both in our early thirties but I am worried that after three kids and ten years with me, he'll run off with a younger woman. Should I marry him?

– C.M., France

Dear C.M.,

Economists have gathered evidence from speed-dating and internet dating, and found that it supports the conventional wisdom: men like young women and women like rich men. Clearly, you have reason to be nervous.

I keep re-reading your letter and I cannot work out whether you regard the risk of desertion as a reason to get married or a reason not to. No matter: a spot of game theory, which economists use to understand how rational people interact with each other, may help you here. You have three options: dump him now; stay with him but do not get married; or get married now. Ten years later he will respond by staying with you or leaving you for the nanny.

Dumping him seems odd: you already have a child together, you enjoy the relationship, and dumping him will not change the unpleasant logic of evolutionary psychology, which puts you at an increasing disadvantage as you both grow older. Staying with him seems more sensible, but if he does run off you will have limited negotiating power. Marrying him seems best of all: the legal contract, in most jurisdictions, protects you against this sort of behaviour. You cannot prevent him leaving you, but you can make it an expensive proposition for him if it happens.

Do I hear the distant sound of wedding bells? Happy Valentine's Day.

Yours matrimonially,
The Undercover Economist

I am a third-year university student and I share a flat with a student on the same course as me from the year below. We are good friends, but I, alas, want us to be more than that. The risks of my confessing my feelings are quite high. If it works out, I have a girlfriend; if it doesn't, I'll end up homeless, looking for an (almost prohibitively expensive one-person) apartment, having lost my best friend. If I keep her in the dark I'm guaranteed to have a roof over my head for the two remaining years. Can economics provide an answer to my dilemma?

– Unnamed student, London

Dear Student,

The cost-benefit analysis here is deceptive, so let me walk you through it. Your mistake has been to frame your dilemma as a static choice problem: either you confess now and take your chances, or you never confess.

That is wrong. There is, dare I say it, a third way. Simply wait and see whether anything is clearer tomorrow, or the next day, or the day after that.

In technical terms, you have an option on making a pass at this lucky lady, and you will continue to have that option until either you actually do so, or until either you or she falls for someone else. The option is valuable and should not be exercised lightly, and thus expended. Option valuation models suggest that you should make your move only if you are absolutely sure (you clearly are not) or if other suitors are circling and your option is about to vanish anyway.

Even in the latter circumstance, you shouldn't make your

move if you feel the odds are against you. I suspect they are. The chances are that this young woman knows exactly how you feel. Since she has done nothing to encourage you, I expect she is praying you'll keep your feelings to yourself.

Yours with options,
The Undercover Economist

Dear Undercover Economist,

Finding myself alone again, I have joined a dating agency. As a result, I am taking delightful, unattached women out to dinner. This is almost always very enjoyable and, according to tradition, I pay for the meal. I am very happy to do this but I am disappointed when the woman in question does not send me a text or other message the next morning to say thank you. Am I expecting too much in this modern world?

– R.S., London

Dear R.S.,

Oh dear. I am inclined to agree that a thank you is appropriate, and if you are not receiving so much as a text or an email, this is a bad sign. But a sign of what?

Scenario one: the woman is a rational self-interested agent. If she regarded a free dinner as sufficient compensation for the time she had to spend in your company, then a 'thank you' would be a simple way of securing a repeat of the experience. The fact such gratitude is not forthcoming suggests your dining companion did not wish for a second date. Nor did she care if you regarded her as ungrateful or said so to others. In short, she would be happy never to see you again.

Scenario two: your date wished to continue the relationship, but was too stupid or self-obsessed to realise that 'thank you' would be a good first step. In which case, you are better off without her.

A final possibility is that your offer to pay for dinner struck your companion as sexist. But then, either she protested and you boorishly ignored her, in which case scenario one now applies (you have no chance); or she let you pay anyway and then sulked, in which case scenario two applies (you got away lightly).

The good news? You seem to enjoy these first-date dinners – and I suspect many more are in prospect.

Yours gratefully,
The Undercover Economist

Dear Undercover Economist,

I was recently stood up on a first date. The guy sent me a message four hours after we were supposed to meet, saying he hadn't made it because he'd had to work and had been unable to call because his phone battery was dead. I was disappointed and angry. When he apologised and proposed meeting up later that week, I said no.

I found these excuses all too familiar. Using 'working' as an excuse without respecting my time was exactly what my ex-boyfriend did to me. I always forgave him, and tried to be understanding. But he did this repeatedly and each time he knew that I was going to forgive him. Never again!

However, maybe everyone needs a chance to make things right. Am I punishing this guy for my ex's behaviour?

– B.C.

Dear B.C.,

This is an experimentation problem: how much do you need to see of a man's behaviour before deciding you'd be better off without him? It is also a signalling problem: you need to ensure you don't appear to be a doormat.

With your ex-boyfriend, you made both mistakes: ignoring plentiful evidence of his selfishness, while encouraging him to walk all over you by forgiving his abuse. (Economists call this latter problem 'moral hazard'.)

Yet I think you have been harsh on the new chap. Admittedly, he got off to a poor start.

If you have a queue of suitors, by all means move on. If not, it would be wise to allow him one chance. Your 'no second chances' policy gives him the right incentives in future, but that is irrelevant unless you give him another try.

You should make the price of a second date high but not infinite. Insist on lobster and champagne. If he complies, he has made it worth your while. He will also have learned to keep his phone charged in future.

Yours tardily,
The Undercover Economist

Money For Good Marks

Work, School and Money

Dear Undercover Economist,

My son has two children and my daughter four. I propose
to give £5,000 to each grandchild in my will. Would this
be equitable, given that £20,000 would go to my
daughter's side of the family and only £10,000 to my
son's?

– Mr Robinson

Dear Mr Robinson,

Let me be frank: at first glance I thought your dilemma was idi-
otic. If you want to hand out equal shares, that's fine – but make
your mind up. Given your daughter's fecundity and some basic
arithmetic it is quite clear that you cannot simultaneously give
equal shares to grandchildren and to children.

Why, then, would you hand out £5,000 to each grandchild and
still fret about fairness between your children? Your children
don't get the money; your grandchildren do. Similarly, it would
make no sense to hand out £15,000 to each child and then start
worrying that your grandchildren had been unequally treated.

Yet arch-rationalists such as Gary Becker or Robert Barro
might leap to your defence. Assume your children are Becker-
Barro altruists. This means that they care not about how much
cash they give, but about the total sum their children receive
from all sources.

If you give your grandchildren £5,000 each, that is simply
£5,000 that their parents don't have to give. They will adjust their
bequests in the light of yours. Viewed in this way, your attempts

to give money to your grandchildren are really hidden transfers to your children – and you would be quite right to worry that your daughter was getting more than your son.

But before you pat yourself on the back (Becker has a Nobel prize; Barro may get one too), ask yourself if your children *are* Becker-Barro altruists. Most people focus narrowly on their bequests, not on the total receipts of their offspring. I doubt your children are Becker-Barro altruists. After all, you aren't.

Yours even-handedly,
The Undercover Economist

Dear Undercover Economist,

Samantha, my PA, is so very unreliable. For example, she failed to pass on your invitation to feature as a responding correspondent in your recent 'Dear Undercover Economist' plug article. However, she does have a fantastic pair of, er . . . feet. Should I fire her?

– Bob Casablanca

Dear Mr Casablanca,

Much depends on your line of business. In Mel Brooks's masterpiece, *The Producers*, the crooked Broadway magnate Max Bialystock hires a blonde bombshell, Ulla, whose secretarial skills consist solely of the ability to pick up the telephone and intone, '*Bialystock unt Bloom, Good tag por day.*' She can, however, dance.

Bialystock is happy enough, which is understandable given that the sole aim of his production is to go bankrupt.

It is unlikely that you share Bialystock's aims, but if you work for a large organisation, you may share his contempt for his shareholders. Your PA's incompetence largely disadvantages them, while her aesthetic appeal – which an economist might call a 'non-pecuniary benefit' – is enjoyed by you alone.

Naturally you have to ensure that your PA's failings are not so disastrous as to damage your own career, but that should be manageable, especially if you continue blaming her whenever something goes wrong.

If you own a large stake in the business, the trade-off is more painful. Samantha will be costing you money. I cannot advise you as to the right course of action, since I don't know how much money you have, how much you want, and how 'fantastic' she really is. I would simply note that you can always look for other options. You could hire a second PA to work in parallel with Samantha. Or you could seek out a PA who offers the best of everything. It cannot be impossible to find an assistant who is both effective and attractive.

Yours ornamentally,
The Undercover Economist

———————

Dear Undercover Economist,

My husband and I are following a tight budget, whereby he is using an Excel spreadsheet to plan our gas usage, spending of store-card loyalty points, and so on. (I name just two of the twelve columns.) However, I became concerned when I lost a glove and its value was inputted into the 'deficit' column – aptly titled Column Thirteen.

I challenged this, as the glove was singular and therefore half the cost.

It was also actually a gift – or two gifts. Are we down £15 (the approximate price of the pair of gloves), down £7.50, up £7.50, or quids in? This has become a sensitive issue in our marriage.

– Mrs, soon-to-be-Miss

Dear soon-to-be-Miss,

That the gloves were a gift is no longer important: the question is whether you are worse off for having lost them. And you are. Nor are you worse off by a mere half-pair of gloves. Your gloves are, in the jargon, perfect or near-perfect complements. This means that the odd glove is worth little, unless you are holding down a career as a Michael Jackson impersonator. The missing glove will be difficult to replace. Your husband is right to claim that you have, in effect, lost the full pair of gloves.

But your husband's competence ends there.

His 'deficit' column makes no sense in a spreadsheet designed to track expenditure. If you buy a replacement pair of gloves, then that is the moment to make a note in your spreadsheet, not before. You may not feel the need to replace them; it is August, after all.

Let's be honest, though. This isn't about the gloves, is it? It's about your husband's infuriating attempt to control you through a spreadsheet.

Tell him either to put it away, or to add Column Fourteen: divorce expenses.

Yours with iron fist in expensive glove,
The Undercover Economist

Dear Undercover Economist,

In the bunfight for Christmas leave, it's never too early to start. I work in middle office, where there is an operational requirement to be staffed to a minimum of 50 per cent at all times. This year there are three working days between Christmas and New Year, and nobody wants to work them. What is the fairest way of divvying up the Christmas leave?

– Middle Office Minion, London

Dear Minion,

It is an outrage that you and your colleagues have been placed in this absurd position. Let's review the facts: you place a higher value on your time between Christmas and New Year, but your company's annual leave policy does not place a higher price on these days. Given this pricing policy, everybody wants leave at Christmas, and so a bureaucratic bodge job is duly handed down from on high.

It is as though the company had offered each staff member a Christmas gift of either a bottle of champagne or a can of lager, and then started inventing rules on discovering that there was not enough champagne for everyone. The idiots who foisted this system on you should scrap it at once, and instead offer sufficient overtime pay at Christmas to ensure that there are enough recruits.

Failing that, the sensible solution is to arrange side-payments among yourselves. The people who value the break least (those with different faiths, or infuriating relatives) should be the ones doing Christmas duty, while the rest pay them compensation. Arrange a quick auction in which the amount of compensation rises over time; when enough bidders have dropped out of the auction, the remaining bidders pay the volunteers to hold the fort. Perhaps the compensation should be suitably seasonal: the bidding could open at one partridge in a pear tree.

Yours festively,
The Undercover Economist

Dear Undercover Economist,

Thanks to the recession kindly engineered by financial whizz-kids, I find myself jobless with large debts and a house that is worth less than the mortgage. I have some redundancy money. What am I supposed to do with it? It's not enough to pay off my debts. Financial disaster seems very likely, so why shouldn't I just spend the windfall on lottery tickets?

– J.P., via email

Dear J.P.,

I'm not going to argue with you about the expected returns on lottery tickets; you'll know that your chances of winning anything worthwhile are near zero. Let me make a more striking claim: even if you won, it would be unlikely to save you from financial trouble.

The economists Scott Hankins, Mark Hoekstra and Paige Marta Skiba are in the process of investigating that claim, looking at 35,000 winners of the Florida lottery, almost 2,000 of whom later filed for bankruptcy. The researchers find that lottery winners are more likely to go bankrupt than others – which is not surprising, since many of them don't win much, and lottery enthusiasts tend to be poor.

More surprising is the discovery that those who won between $50,000 and $150,000 were as likely to have gone bankrupt five years later as those who won less than $10,000. Since the size of a win is random, there should have been no difference between big winners and small winners at the time they bought their ticket. It is remarkable that the additional money was not used to pay off debts.

Admittedly, winning $100,000 did seem to postpone bankruptcy by a year or two, so presumably these winners had a nice time on their way to ruin. Yet this is not an approach I feel able to recommend. Finding a job would go a long way to solving your problems. I won't pretend that will be easy, but the odds are better than those of winning the lottery.

Yours conscientiously,
The Undercover Economist

Dear Undercover Economist,

With the economy slowing down, I have seen an outburst of 'pay-what-you-want' options where customers of, say, coffee shops are encouraged to pay what they consider the product or service is truly worth. Is this sustainable in the long term, or will people take advantage of it, gaming the system into failure?

– John Wegman, London

Dear John,

While we economists realise that people pay money even when they don't legally have to, few of us have studied exactly when or why. One exception is Paul F., the 'bagel man' made famous by Stephen J. Dubner and Steven D. Levitt, the authors of *Freakonomics*. Paul F., a retired economist, delivered bagels to offices, along with a box for payment. He specified prices and kept careful track of payment rates – a little under ninety per cent.

Pay-what-you-want goes further than this simple honesty system, and might work better because it stands a chance of persuading affluent customers to pay over the odds. Most retailers devote great ingenuity to this task of 'price discrimination'; it would simplify things a lot if customers simply complied.

Yet I am doubtful. A major attraction of pay-what-you-want is free publicity, whether for an ageing rock band or the new café on the block. The more businesses try it, the less publicity each will receive. I wonder, too, whether customers continue to contribute more than they must after the thrill of the new wears off: the economists John List and Uri Gneezy once conducted an experiment to see if temporary workers tried harder if unexpectedly paid a generous wage. The answer: yes, but the gratitude wears off in a matter of hours.

Still, pay-what-you-want has to be worth a try. If the journalists look elsewhere and the customers become ungrateful, it's a simple matter to install a cash register.

Yours for whatever your want,
The Undercover Economist

Dear Undercover Economist,

Our son (aged fourteen) has been going to a local school and has made friends and settled in. But we are not happy. We think the school is poor, with a high teacher turnover, low expectations, poor exam grades and now a bad report from school inspectors. We're thinking of moving him to a different school but we don't want to disrupt his education. What should we do?

– John and Julia, London

Dear John and Julia,

The economists Eric A. Hanushek, John Kain and Steven Rivkin have looked at data on Texas schools. They conclude that moving children repeatedly is disruptive both to the child and to his peers, but that a one-off move causes only temporary disruption to studies, especially if carried out at the end of an academic year. The researchers also found that in the cases where children were moved to better schools, they achieved a lasting improvement in academic performance.

A similar conclusion emerges from the research of another economist, Bruce Sacerdote, who looked into the aftermath of the Katrina disaster. After Hurricanes Katrina and Rita, about 200,000 Louisiana children had to switch schools. Unsurprisingly, test scores took a sharp turn for the worse. Yet Sacerdote finds that for those evacuees who left schools in urban New Orleans, which had a terrible reputation, test scores recovered within two years. College enrolment rates also improved. Three years after the disruption, children who began in bad schools ended up doing better than if Katrina had never struck.

My conclusion is that your son can thrive after a school move, but only if the new school really is superior. I am not sure what criteria you used to select the current one, but you might want to revise them before choosing the next. If I was your son, I'd be wondering why you think you will be second time lucky.

Yours educationally,
The Undercover Economist

Dear Undercover Economist,

I work with an international bank, but have recently been laid off. Fortunately, I have managed to land myself another job in this very tough job market (yes, in India too!).

The catch is that my current employer is offering me a severance package of around twenty months pay – but only if I stick around for six more weeks, while the other company wants me to join as soon as possible.

One option gives me a pile of hard cash, but uncertainty and the stigma of unemployment. The other option is a secure and cushy job. And, another thing: India does not have any unemployment benefits.

– P.M., India

Dear P.M.,

I'm not surprised you're tempted by the severance package, especially with two companies fighting over which employs you for the next six weeks – a great boost to your ego.

Still, I'd urge you not to get too confident. An economics PhD student at MIT, Johannes Spinnewijn, recently published a research paper showing that most unemployed people are too cocky about their prospects of finding a new job. On average, they expect seven weeks of unemployment, but eventually endure twenty-three weeks. And this is using data from the mid-1990s, not recession years. Be warned, then: don't let overconfidence lure you into undervaluing the guarantee of a good job.

A better approach would be to negotiate a compromise. Surely there is a way to secure the new job without losing all the severance pay – perhaps involving part-time work for both companies for the next two months.

If you do decide to turn down the new job and look again with severance pay in hand, look very hard indeed. Spinnewijn's research shows that job-seekers tend to harbour another misperception: that an energetic job search does not pay dividends. They are wrong.

Yours proactively,
The Undercover Economist

Dear Undercover Economist,

Should my co-workers and I accept a pay cut to preserve our jobs?

– David A., London

Dear David A.,

In principle, of course you should: this is so obvious that I'm not even sure why you bothered to ask. Another way of phrasing this question is to ask whether you would rather have most of your old salary or none of it.

You might object that unemployment has one big advantage over a pay cut: it means that you don't have to work. For most people, however, this is not an advantage. The economist Andrew Oswald, one of a growing clan of 'happiness economists', has found that unemployment is extremely distressing, far more than could be explained by mere financial loss. If he is right, jobs bring happiness and self-respect, and even a severe pay cut is worth taking on the chin if that's what it takes to stay in work.

It is true that taking a pay cut may result in a lower salary for many years, but losing your job, especially in a recession, is worse: your skills depreciate rapidly and you are quite likely to be worse off for the rest of your life.

You might reasonably ask why it isn't more common to see swingeing pay cuts in place of redundancies. They are preferable for employees and probably preferable for employers, too. After all, sacking people is costly, as is going short-staffed and re-hiring people when things pick up. Far better just to squeeze salaries.

But that's too easy. I suspect that there is a strong bias against salary cuts because otherwise employers would be demanding them every couple of weeks, with the flimsiest of excuses. Sacking somebody, in contrast, is not something an employer will tend to do lightly.

That is why 'either pay me properly or sack me' is a good negotiating position. But, like many good negotiating positions, it may occasionally backfire.

Yours inexpensively,
The Undercover Economist

Dear Undercover Economist,

I have worked full-time for six years and presently earn £40,000. I am also about to attain chartered engineer status, which sounds good. However, I stumbled on an old letter the other day that confirmed my admission into nursery aged four, twenty-nine years ago! Looking back at all the money invested in my more than twenty years of formal education, I feel short-changed by my income and quality of life.

Do you know how I can calculate a 'fair' figure that will reflect my master's degree and international experience? I want to use this as the minimum salary for my next job.

– G

Dear G,

I'm not going to attempt to calculate your 'fair' figure: it would do you no good. Employers care very little about what salary would be a fair reward for your background; instead, they want the best possible people for the lowest possible cost. Competition from other employers typically leads them to compromise on both counts.

Your fair figure might eat away still further at your fading happiness. It seems that you were satisfied until you reflected on your education and inflated your aspirations. This is sad but typical, if the economist Andrew Oswald is to be believed.

Oswald has compared people's circumstances with their happiness. He finds that, other things being equal, happiness rises with money, good health and a successful marriage, but falls as a person's 'expected income' rises. Expected income is the income that another person of the same age, sex and education level would typically earn. In other words, more educated people have richer peers and so tend to be less satisfied.

What is especially sad is that your income would comfortably put you in the richest ten per cent of UK citizens, who are themselves relatively rich. As for being short-changed, I doubt that you personally paid for your nursery education. Put away your admission letter, and forget about it.

Yours unfairly,
The Undercover Economist

Dear Undercover Economist,

I struggle to wake up in the morning although I sleep, on average, seven and a half hours. As I do have a flexible timetable, I arrive at work at 10 a.m. I would like to start at 9 a.m., but my laziness makes it impossible.

Do you have any advice?

– Ruth

Dear Ruth,

Your guide here must be the Nobel laureate Thomas Schelling. Schelling's expertise as a game theorist was honed by his experiences as a cold war strategist – he advised John F. Kennedy during the Berlin crisis.

Schelling realised that the same bargaining and bluffing techniques that worked against Nikita Khrushchev might also work in an individual's struggle with herself, to quit smoking, diet or get out of bed in the morning. He called the idea 'egonomics'.

Your predicament is a contest between two competitors, Evening Ruth and Morning Ruth. Evening Ruth has fine ideas about an early start, but her late nights impose costs on Morning Ruth, who then stays in bed.

One option is to tie Morning Ruth's hands, just as Odysseus ordered his sailors to tie him to the mast. Evening Ruth might buy one of those motorised alarm clocks that falls off the dresser and scuttles under the bed, beeping loudly.

An alternative is to recruit a third player. The British government handed over control of interest rates to the Bank of England. Similarly, ask an early-bird friend to call every morning.

Odder still, Evening Ruth could enlist Bad Cop Ruth to punish Morning Ruth for lie-ins by, say, denying her(self) television privileges. Bizarre as it may seem to turn one person's decision into a three-way inner struggle, Schelling avers that this technique works.

One final point. Your letter was evidently composed by Evening Ruth. Are you sure that Morning Ruth's preferences are so mistaken?

Yours punctually,
The Undercover Economist

———————

Dear Undercover Economist,

Being a considerate father, I am planning a monetary incentive scheme to improve my eighteen-year-old son's marks at school. Instead of executing a relative's bequest as decreed, I intend to spend the €7,000 rewarding good results. During three semesters, he will have to pass forty-eight preliminary tests, then the main exams in the fourth and last semester. How should I divide up the capital?

– Robert Saverin, a grateful father

Dear Mr Saverin,

Start by promising more than you can deliver. If you offer €10,000 for a perfect score, you will only need to apologise after your scheme has succeeded. That may seem to undermine your credibility, but the real risk lies the other way: your son may expect to get the money from his doting dad anyway. Discourage this view or your plan will be in vain.

You must also pitch the stakes just right. Research in behavioural economics suggests that trivial rewards are worse than no rewards, but also that performance suffers when too much is at stake.

Finally, focus on the early exams, because success breeds success. Promise your son €200 for every excellent result in these: that should engage his interest without throwing him into a panic. If things go well, the money will run out before the high-pressure exams. But by then he will have mastered his subjects anyway.

Your friendly pedagogue,
The Undercover Economist

Dear Undercover Economist,

My four-year-old son has a July birthday, which would make him one of the youngest in his class at school. I am thinking of keeping him back a year so that when he does start school, he'll be bigger and more confident. Is this a good idea?

– Sarah Goldberg, by email

Dear Sarah,

Other parents think it is. The economists David Deming and Susan Dynarski have found that the percentage of six-year-olds not yet registered at school has quadrupled in the US over the past forty years, largely because parents are holding back their children.

Being older seems to convey lasting benefits in sports: an unusual number of international footballers are old for their year, for instance. That is surely because the older children are more likely to be selected for the most competitive games with the best coaches. Academic streaming may create a similar effect.

An influential piece of research, from Kelly Bedard and Elizabeth Dhuey (also economists), found that the oldest in the class tended to do better not just when five or six but even as college students.

Not every study agrees, and Deming and Dynarski also point out that starting school late has its costs. Still, one thing is certain: since your boy has a mother who is fussing about this sort of stuff, he's going to do fine no matter what.

Yours from a September baby,
The Undercover Economist

How to Wear the Trousers

Family Life

Dear Undercover Economist,

My newly-wed wife and I are deeply in love. There is, however, one issue that threatens the blissful fabric of our marriage. I absolutely insist upon shopping at Wal-Mart. My wife, meanwhile, would rather avoid Wal-Mart at all costs.

I have recently tried to convince her that not only does Wal-Mart offer the lowest prices known to man, but that the chain is also a force for good – lower prices mean better standards of living for all consumers, increased global trade means a tighter-knit international community, and efficient operations translate into higher productivity growth for the economy. My wife complains about poor labour policies, the 'fact' that Wal-Mart squeezes suppliers, and that it puts local shops out of business.

Who is right? Will our marriage survive?

– Brian Gee

Dear Brian,

I have to agree with you about Wal-Mart. Jason Furman, then an economist at New York University, now an adviser to President Obama, famously argued in 2005 that Wal-Mart was (unwittingly) a progressive success story. The chain's prices don't much affect me (I prefer Whole Foods) but Furman reckoned that they benefited low- and middle-income Americans to the tune of around $250 billion a year.

Wal-Mart does not pay much, so it may depress wages. Then again, it may boost wages by offering jobs to the otherwise unemployed. Either way, the benefits of low prices to Wal-Mart shoppers far outweigh any plausible costs to Wal-Mart employees. And while it is true that Wal-Mart employees tend to be poor, the same is true of Wal-Mart shoppers.

Armed with this information you can confront your wife with confidence. You are sure to win the conversation. The divorce is likely to be more keenly contested.

Yours at a cut-price rate,
The Undercover Economist

Dear Undercover Economist,

My fifteen-year-old is disinclined to work for her GCSEs, saying her time is better spent preening herself in preparation for assignations with her delightful, diligent, privately educated, moneyed boyfriend. She insists the money spent on nail-painting, hair-colouring and the like is an investment and will be more than repaid when he marries her. Is she deluding herself?

– A curious mother

Dear Curious Mother,

Surprising as this may seem in the twenty-first century, your daughter's strategy is not unusual. Evidence on speed-dating gathered by the economists Michèle Belot and Marco Francesconi shows that women are attracted by rich men, while men focus more on a woman's physical appearance. Lena Edlund, another economist, has found that in the areas of her native Sweden where the wealthiest men live, women of prime marriageable age are over-represented.

However, your daughter is only fifteen; for Edlund, 'prime marriageable age' is 25–44. Your daughter is either going to have to get her hooks into this chap unusually early, or she is going to have to keep him on the boil for another decade – a lot of nail-painting.

Not only is she concentrating her investments into a single asset by abandoning her education, but she may even be making her main goal harder to achieve. Belot and Francesconi discovered that a strong social trend towards 'assortative mating' means that although educated, high-achieving men are not interested in marrying a rich woman, they do like educated high-achieving women, rather than shallow girls with shiny nails.

Your daughter should learn to work hard and look good at the same time. Not only will it advance her immediate goals, it will also – sadly – stand her in good stead for the rest of her life.

Yours decoratively,
The Undercover Economist

———————

Dear Undercover Economist,

Having become more computer-literate in recent months, I have made an unpleasant discovery. My husband has been visiting pornographic websites and has also downloaded explicit videos. I love my husband, but am not sure what to do now. Is his behaviour common?

– Katie Durlap, Cincinnati, Ohio

Dear Katie,

If only you had a subscription to the *Journal of Economic Perspectives*. One of its regular features is a data-driven description of different markets in action, most recently a study by Benjamin Edelman asking 'Who buys online adult entertainment?'

The latest data reported are from 2006, when adult entertainment clocked up $13 billion in retail sales in the US – about $50 per adult, presumably somewhat skewed towards men. Much of this was video sales and rentals, but internet and cable subscriptions are also substantial and, unlike video, growing briskly.

Paid subscriptions to internet porn sites remain a minority hobby. Edelman studied subscriptions to one top-ten service provider and found that almost all states had between two and three subscribers per 1,000 home broadband users. Ohio, incidentally, is towards the low end of that range.

Is your husband, then, unusual? Not that unusual. Scale up Edelman's numbers to include other service providers, add cable subscriptions and you'd conclude that about five per cent of connected households are paying for regular porn. This doesn't include the largest category, video rental – and more importantly, doesn't include free internet porn. Since free internet porn is ubiquitous and presumably more private, one can only surmise that it is far more widespread.

I can't tell you what to do about your husband – but he is certainly not alone.

Explicitly yours,
The Undercover Economist

Dear Undercover Economist,

Although Christmas in the company of various members of the extended family was fun, it was interrupted and spoiled by family rows over who got to watch what television programme, who got the best seat, who did the washing-up, and so on. Can economics prevent such rows spoiling next Christmas?

– Penny Belton, Gloucester

Dear Penny,

I am all in favour of assigning clear property rights in such cases. Someone can 'own' the right to the remote control; the best seat can also go up for grabs, as can exemption from the washing-up rota.

One can get pretty fancy about these auctions, but I wouldn't advise doing so unless you're going to buy bespoke software and hire a team of specialist economists. A simple set of auctions for temporary use of selected scarce resources should do the trick.

I have made this sort of recommendation before on the basis

of sound economic theory. This year, I am delighted to report that I have empirical support. Bev Stewart, a grandmother from Yorkshire, auctioned the right to spend Boxing Day in the comfy armchair in front of the telly. All family members were eligible to bid; she was expecting a 'rabble of Stewarts' to descend upon her the day after Christmas.

The winner, after seventeen bids from a range of bidders, was her daughter-in-law for the sum of £13.50. The ingenious Grandma Stewart not only raised money for a good cause, but prevented the annual arguments over what she is quoted as saying is the 'perfect seat . . . straight in front of the TV and has got the coffee table at the side for you to rest your drink on and the TV remote, so everybody wants to sit there'.

Twenty-five family members and no arguments. If auctions can work for Bev Stewart, they can work for us all.

Yours seasonally,
The Undercover Economist

———————

Dear Undercover Economist,

I am a father of three teenagers and happily married for almost twenty years. In my opinion the secret to my success is a traditional one, which is that there is no doubt about who wears the trousers. I am wondering whether there is any support in economic theory for my view?

– Harry R., Surrey

Dear Harry,

There is ample support in economic theory for your view – it is just a shame there is little support for it in practice. Economists have always tended to use a 'household' model of decision-making, which treats domestic decisions as being made by one person – the kind of benign dictator with whom you, as paterfamilias, identify yourself. This had the chief virtue of simplicity.

Gary Becker, a Nobel laureate, then advocated treating the household as if it had more than one decision-maker. This helped to explain rococo details such as the existence of divorce lawyers.

Changes that increased the bargaining power of women, such as the introduction of 'no fault' divorce, turned out to have the logical consequence that women became less likely to be physically abused by husbands. They also reduced the likelihood that couples would invest in each other – for example, by financially supporting one partner through a professional course.

The plot now thickens. The economist William T. Harbaugh, with colleagues, has discovered that children as young as eleven seem to make rational consumption choices as well as adults do. And a team including the economist Anyck Dauphin has demonstrated that British teenagers do influence household consumption, especially if they have access to their own income. The paterfamilias household is no more.

How, then, should we reconcile this with your own situation, which seems comfortably wedged in the 1950s? My guess is that your wife and children have decided that it suits them to maintain your delusions of control.

Yours paternalistically,
The Undercover Economist

———

Disciplining children seems simple enough. Reward them when they do well and punish them when they misbehave. They should respond to incentives, right? Am I missing something?

– Tom Cookson, Berkshire

Dear Tom,

You are right up to a point. Children do respond to incentives, but there are limits to this strategy, the most obvious being that children are impatient. If you cannot help them to become pleasant people without rewards and punishments, you will find that both carrot and stick must be brandished with alarming frequency.

A second problem is credibility. Will you really carry out your threat to subject four-year-old Billy to waterboarding? It seems unlikely, and since Billy will not always respond to your threats, he will soon discover if they are hollow.

The challenge, then, is to make sure that you have punishments available to you that you are willing to carry out. You may be able to rise to that challenge by building up what Joshua Gans calls 'punishment capital' – not to be confused with capital punishment. Professor Gans, author of a new book called *Parentonomics*, points out that if you are the source of a steady stream of money or sweets, that gives you a negotiating position. Threatening to remove the carrot (or rather, the flow of chocolate coins) is more credible than threatening to wield the stick. What one parent sees as junk food, Professor Gans sees as an 'incentive opportunity'.

I have written before about the research of economist Bruce

Weinberg, who finds that children in richer families are much less likely to be spanked, yet more likely to have allowances withdrawn. That makes sense: poor families lack all kinds of capital, and that includes punishment capital too.

Yours indulgently,
The Undercover Economist

Dear Undercover Economist,

I have recently agreed with my student partner that she will move into my flat during the Edinburgh Festival so that she can sublet her room and pay for her half of our holiday together. She maintains that she should pay me for staying in the flat, whereas I argue that this would defeat the purpose of the exercise. How can we effectively resolve this dispute and look forward to our holiday? Should I simply charge her for any increase in my bills, or are there other considerations?

– Ben, Edinburgh

Dear Ben,

Stop the tiptoeing about who pays what to whom. Let's be blunt: she can't afford this holiday, you can afford to subsidise her, but she doesn't seem to want to incur too large a debt. It seems to me there are two solutions: an explicit contract, or an implicit one.

The implicit contract: quietly subsidise her holiday. Accept a little money from her as a tenant, and pick up a few of the extra holiday costs. The explicit contract: charge her the market rate for staying in your flat. Do not be surprised, however, if she begins to charge you for 'services' provided either during her stay or on your holiday.

Choose whichever contract is to your taste. It will set the tone for your relationship – and the explicit contract may be cheaper in the long run.

Yours explicitly,
The Undercover Economist

———————

Dog Food Versus Spam

Food, Drink and Entertainment

Dear Undercover Economist,

After reading with interest your plan to start exercising last Christmas (by giving to charity if you didn't meet your goals), I'd be obliged if you could offer an opinion on a similar scheme I have concocted. Wine is the problem. I drink too much of the glorious stuff, and am unable to convince myself that doing so is unhealthy.

Your idea of giving to charity would not work with me: I'm uncharitable, I'm afraid, and would probably rather lie than give my earnings away. Here is my alternative. Each month I will deposit the total amount I would spend on wine in the family joint bank account. If I want a bottle, it must come out of this account, but whatever is left at the end of the month is to be given to my wife and children.

This appears to be an excellent solution; in my view, the guilt of taking something away from my beloved wife and children is far greater than taking from myself. Do you agree?

– D.W.

Dear D.W.,

In classical economic theory, your scheme would be useless. Every pound spent on the demon drink is always a pound unavailable to your wife and children, and it should make no difference which bank account you put it in.

But Richard Thaler, a leading behavioural economist, has a theory of 'mental accounting' that supports your plan. We do attach different labels to different pounds: this one is for my pension, that one is slush money. And Thaler has discovered that those labels make a difference to the way we behave.

Your scheme may well work, then. But like all commitment strategies, there is a risk that it will backfire, and you end up with the worst of all worlds. You may find yourself unable to stop drinking, feel more guilty than ever, and demonstrate unambiguously to your family that you love booze more than you love them. You evidently like to live dangerously: good luck.

Yours bibulously,
The Undercover Economist

Dear Undercover Economist,

In your books and columns you have claimed that when people split the bill equally in restaurants they tend to take advantage of each other by ordering expensive dishes. I wonder if this is really true. Wouldn't friends be more considerate of each other?

– Considerate restaurant-goer, London

Dear CRG,

The 'diner's dilemma' you describe is a kind of prisoner's dilemma, and in theory people should behave exactly as I have described. But many laboratory experiments suggest we are not as selfish as economists' models claim. So you are right to ask for more evidence.

The economists Uri Gneezy, Ernan Haruvy and Hadas Yafe have been looking into this. They seated various groups of six diners at a nice restaurant in Haifa, Israel, and noted how they responded to different payment schemes. Some ate for free, and they ordered a lot. Others paid for their own order, and they ordered sparingly. Between those two extremes were those who split the bill with the other five diners: they took advantage of their fellow diners, as I would have expected.

Perhaps they were somewhat inhibited by the embarrassment of free-riding, though? It seems not. When the experimenters, in a further trial, told diners that they would pay one-sixth of their individual bill only, they faced the same costs of over-ordering as in the 'split the bill' case, but if they made extravagant choices their dining companions did not suffer. Yet they ordered much the same as in the 'split the bill' case, suggesting that saving money for fellow diners was not much of a consideration.

It's worth emphasising that this experiment seated strangers together, not friends. Perhaps people are more generous when it comes to friends. Or perhaps they are simply more careful about their reputations.

Yours magnanimously,
The Undercover Economist

Dear Undercover Economist,

You have advised readers that, in blind tests, most people like the taste of inexpensive wine, and that their impressions of wine are more closely correlated with the price tag than with expert opinion. In other words, it is possible to save money by drinking plonk. In these straitened times, can we draw similar conclusions about food?

– Harry Nicholas, Los Angeles

Dear Harry,

My gurus in these matters are the members of the American Association of Wine Economists, and a new AAWE working paper, 'Can people distinguish pâté from dog food?', suggests an answer to your question. The authors were the 'Gonzo Scientist' John Bohannon and two food critics who had worked on the earlier findings on cheap wine.

The appearance of food is key, so it was an important breakthrough to realise that dog food and pâté look much the same – once the former has been blended to a mousse-like consistency and garnished with parsley. In order to win over some subjects without deceit, the experimenters began with a wine-tasting session. Subjects were then offered two quality pâtés, two cheap imitations (puréed liverwurst and puréed spam) and the dog food – all accompanied by Carr's water biscuits.

The results were surprising. Subjects overwhelmingly rated Dish C (the dog food) as the least tasty. However, few actually thought Dish C contained dog food. Broadly, people thought that Dish E (the liverwurst) was the dog food; they also thought it tasted good. Disappointingly, most people correctly identified the expensive pâtés, and the blind-taste rankings correlated exactly with the (unseen) price tags. In other words, there are no bargains to be had by serving dog food to dinner-party guests. No wonder economics is known as the dismal science.

Yours, barking,
The Undercover Economist

———————

Dear Undercover Economist,

As a wine evangelist, I always bring a bottle of something really decent whenever I visit friends. The trouble is, their thanks rarely reflect my expenditure. Should I make more of a fuss about the cost of fine wine, or just bring plonk?

– Gabriel Elliott, London

Dear Gabriel,

Either plan would work just fine. Several pieces of research by wine critics and 'neuro-economists' have found that most wine drinkers pay more attention to price than they do to taste.

Research published by the *Journal of Wine Economics* shows that inexpert wine drinkers actually prefer cheap wine in a blind tasting. More skilled oenophiles do prefer pricier booze, but only a little. That suggests you should buy plonk with a nice label and a clear conscience.

The alternative is to point out the expense of the wine. This is crass, but should encourage people to rate it more highly.

Or you could bring plonk but claim it is expensive wine. The 'neuro-economist' Antonio Rangel has found people enjoy wine more if they are told (truthfully or otherwise) it is expensive. Not only do they rate the wine more highly, but their brains seem to process the experience differently.

Your friends probably can't tell the difference between expensive and cheap wine. Exploit that information as you wish.

Yours appreciatively,
The Undercover Economist

Dear Undercover Economist,

While at a recent Elton John concert, I observed a heated altercation between two ladies. The younger lady wanted to stand up, dance and sing along with Elton. The older lady, seated directly behind her, wanted to stay seated, watch the band and enjoy the music. The older lady asked the younger to sit down, but was told that she should also stand up and dance. An argument quickly broke out. Any thoughts on how they might have resolved the conflict without swinging handbags?

– David Walker

Dear David,

I blame Elton John himself, since he apparently did not clearly define property rights, contrary to the recommendations of the great economist Ronald Coase.

Should a concert seat come bundled with the right to get up and dance, the older woman could have offered to pay her tormentor to sit down. Conversely, should a seat come bundled with the right to an unobstructed view, it would have been the younger woman offering the bribe. Either way, the dance would have continued only if the dancer's enjoyment outweighed its victim's frustration. Perhaps the bargaining might also have involved swapping seats?

Sadly, with no clear property rights, there was no basis for a deal. No wonder the night turned out to be all right for fighting.

Yours musically,
The Undercover Economist

———————

Pet Rats, Fake Tan and Christmas Trees in August

Miscellaneous Queries

Dear Undercover Economist,

With the imminent passing of my pet rat I am faced with a lot of grief; he has been a great pet and so I will be more saddened by his passing than if he had been a bad one. My question is: is it possible for the cost (the grief from losing a friend/pet/family member) to outweigh the benefit (the joy gained through time spent with them) and so make the purchase of my pet not worth it, as the net benefit would be negative?

– Ilka

Dear Ilka,

Your ailing rat puts me in mind of a departed sparrow, mourned in verse by Catullus.

But poetic speculation gets us nowhere. Let's head straight to the data. Andrew Oswald, professor of economics at Warwick University, provides the following data points to ponder, based on surveys of life-satisfaction.

Relative to never having been married, being married is worth 0.38 'points' of life satisfaction on a scale of 1–7. Being separated is worth -0.24, widowed -0.19 and divorced -0.09.

This is not much to go on, but it is better than nothing. If we incautiously interpret these numbers as causal – in fact they are merely correlations – then we could conclude that twenty years of marriage is compensation for up to forty years of widowhood. Ten years of marriage more than justifies forty years as a divorcee.

For human marriages, these odds seem pretty good. For a pet rat, less so: the little darlings hit puberty at six weeks and rarely live past three years.

Perhaps you should buy a tortoise next time.

With briefest sympathy,
The Undercover Economist

Dear Undercover Economist,

Should the football authorities put a cap on the total value of players, based on their transfer cost, who can play for a Premier League team in any given match? For example, although a squad might have cost a team £150 million, the cap would mean that they could only use players in a match up to a value of £75 million. This would create a level playing field and prevent wealthy clubs from 'buying' silverware through purchasing the best players.

– Keith Bates

Dear Mr Bates,

Your proposal sounds reasonable, but it is muddled on three counts. First, think of the unintended consequences of your rule. It would favour wealthy clubs with expensive established training academies, because they have a stable of young players who carry no transfer price. You would also discourage clubs from trading players if one club's academy discovers three great goalkeepers. And would music fans be better off if Mick Jagger and Keith Richards were forced to take it in turns to play for the Rolling Stones?

Second, transfer payments are not in fact associated with success on the field. The economist Stefan Szymanski, co-author of *Why England Lose*, has used a statistical analysis to show that while a club's wage bill is correlated with success, its transfer spending is not.

Finally, fans do not actually want a level playing field. Arsenal's 'invincibles' season, 2003–2004, saw them win 84 per cent of league matches and lose none. Every game was a sell-out. More rigorously, Szymanski has shown that more unequal seasons attract more fans. And why not? The big clubs have lots of fans and those fans want to see victories.

In short, you have the wrong objective, suggest the wrong rule to achieve it, and are blind to the side-effects. Any banking regulator in the world would be proud to give you a job.

Your sporting correspondent,
The Undercover Economist

Dear Undercover Economist,

It's that time of year when hemlines get shorter and legs get browner . . . I am having difficulty in achieving an even tan, yet everyone else (bar none!) has a perfect pair of tanned pins. I know they're not natural.

As most men are unfamiliar with the fake tan ritual, let me fill you in. After one has showered, one applies the

cream. The substance comes out of its tube as a cream,
not the colour of 'tan' it will decide to be.

The question is one of when to stop. The tan won't own
up for another four to six hours, so it's a while before I
learn whether the gamble has paid off. When it emerges,
it's patchy and streaky and my knees are two satsumas.
Do I reapply blindly in a bid to colour in the gaps,
risking more streaky satsumas? Or do I wear trousers?

– N.M.

Dear N.M.,

Maybe the whole fake tan business is a game of pure luck, with winners displaying their bronzed legs and unlucky losers resorting to the trouser option. This biased sampling would create the appearance of a world where the ability to apply fake tan is universal.

If this explanation is correct, you must just keep trying and resort to the trousers whenever you fail. But this seems a counsel of despair, and, for reasons that are not purely selfless, I advise against the trousers. You might do better to consult a central banker such as Mervyn King. Extreme monetary policy, such as printing money to buy other assets, is much like applying fake tan. It is all but impossible to know whether you are doing it right at the time, you must wait some time for the results to be apparent, and it is easy to overdo it. I have never seen Mr King's legs up close, but perhaps he is a dab hand with the fake tan. If he is a master of quantitative easing, he may also have perfected quantitative squeezing.

Yours bronzedly,
The Undercover Economist

I wish I frequented the same high street as the statisticians who calculate measures of inflation. Given their calculations include 'Various selected popular brands of sweets, chocolates, gum', will they take note of a Mars Bar shrinking in size from 62.5g to 58g while remaining the same price? I make this an effective price increase of 7.76 per cent. If not, when are those lying bastards going to stop lying to me?

– Ralph Corderoy

Dear Mr Corderoy,

Your arithmetic is correct but your objection is confused. The statisticians – or 'lying bastards', *au choix* – do indeed adjust for such changes. It is far easier for them to do that than to make the many other adjustments they attempt every year to cope with the fact that nobody knows how many gramophones there are in an iPod.

Certainly, you are right to suspect that when the bean-counters go out to calculate inflation, they are not buying exactly the same products that you buy. How could they? Some people spend a lot on petrol, heating and mortgage payments; others are more interested in clothes, fast-food and laptops. The statisticians' best can never be quite good enough.

I will concede, though, that the Mars Bar has been worthy of scrutiny ever since the late Nico Colchester noted in the *Financial Times* back in 1981 that it was a very stable unit of account. It is a veritable ingot of basic commodities (sugar, milk, cocoa) that has kept its value relative to the price of other goods such as small cars, which have cost about 20,000 Mars Bars for the past seventy years.

Fortunately, there is no strong trend towards debasing the Mars Bar – its weight has always fluctuated. It weighed 57g in the late 1970s and as much as 67g in the mid-1980s: 58g is simply a return to historical norms after something of a Mars Bar bubble.

Your confectionate friend,
The Undercover Economist

Dear Undercover Economist,

My tobacco packet has only a helpline number for people who want to quit – not a grotesque picture of the damage caused by smoking-related diseases. This leads me to conclude that I might be prepared to pay more for tobacco if its legally required guilt-trips were in text form, not pictures. Am I on to something?

– Ms Lovegrove, Oxford

Dear Ms Lovegrove,

I think you just might be. The pictures you describe are a form of 'product sabotage', a tactic used by companies with some pricing power. While certain customers are very sensitive to price, others pay less attention. The astute business therefore tries to separate the two and charge them different prices for similar products.

The cheaper product is given some additional defect that the price sensitive customer will swallow and the price-blind customer will not.

Examples abound: Tesco Value products are cheap, but the packaging reminds me of an emergency food drop from the UN. The 'short cappuccino' from Starbucks is cheap – and not advertised on the menu. Most software packages have a cheaper version in which features are disabled at the vendor's expense.

The government could allow the sale of tobacco under two different conditions: the current version, with tax and disturbing pictures; and a 'guilt-free' version with no pictures but a higher tax. The effect would be something to test, but I would expect schoolchildren and the poor to choose the traditional version, while older and more affluent smokers would buy the premium version. I would guess that with two different schemes, the government should be able to discourage more smokers while also raising extra cash. Or perhaps I am just smoking something.

Yours graphically,
The Undercover Economist

Dear Undercover Economist,

When my neighbour was desperately searching for staff to run her guesthouse, I, after due deliberation about whether to get involved and much trouble, eventually found her a married couple who complied with all her demands. She now thanks God for bringing them to her. Do you think she's confusing me with God? If so, should I gently remind her that I'm a simple earthly being and such high praise is making me feel a little uncomfortable? I would prefer you not to use my real name; I don't want any more people contacting me in search of miracles. In any case, my husband thinks this business has gone to my head.

– Mrs S., South Africa

Dear Mrs S.,

I would say that a more likely explanation of your neighbour's actions is that she is trying to ingratiate herself with God, not you. I can imagine how aggravating this is for you, given the trouble you've gone to, but this attitude makes sense if God is subject to flattery. God is, after all, omnipotent, so it must be better to have God on your side than plain Mrs S.

The question is, does God pay attention to supplicants? No less an authority than Nobel laureate James Heckman has investigated the answer using highly fashionable statistical techniques. (Some claim that Heckman's paper is a parody of sloppy statistical practice. I couldn't possibly comment.)

Heckman observes that 'the empirical conclusion from this analysis is important. A little prayer does no good and may make things worse. Much prayer helps a lot.' This is fascinating, suggesting that sit-on-the-fence agnostics are choosing a very foolish approach. Your neighbour has taken this lesson to heart: given the importance of extremely fervent prayer, small wonder that she is giving God all the credit for your hard work.

Yours devoutly,
The Undercover Economist

Should I associate with happy people because they make me feel good by association, or unhappy people because they make me feel good by comparison? Or do economists claim that I should be indifferent?

– D.K., New York

Dear D.K.,

Economic theory makes no such claim: it insists merely that your preferences be consistent and complete because that makes the mathematics easier. Although many economic models concentrate on your demand for physical goods, that is merely to keep things simple. There is no theoretical reason to insist that your happiness cannot depend on the happiness of others.

Your question, then, should be addressed empirically, and a fascinating new paper in the *British Medical Journal* tries to do just that. The authors, James Fowler and Nicholas Christakis, find that happiness is contagious.

If just a single nearby friend becomes happy, your chances of being happy rise by a quarter. Physical proximity seems to be important, and happiness is far more contagious among people of the same sex.

This has a ring of plausibility, yet there are some curious results – for instance, that a happy next-door neighbour seems to affect your mood more than a happy spouse. Meanwhile, in another *BMJ* study, Jason Fletcher and the economist Ethan Cohen-Cole use a similar data set and methodology to demonstrate that height also seems to be contagious, which seems rather unlikely.

The trouble is that it is hard to separate genuine contagion from other effects – such as a shared physical environment, or people befriending others who seem similar to them. My recommendation: by all means seek out happy people, but do not expect miracles.

Yours contentedly,
The Undercover Economist

Dear Undercover Economist,

Due to multiple disruptions to my schedule since the first of the year I have not had the opportunity to take down my Christmas tree. At this point, should I leave the tree up for the remainder of the year or take it down now?

– D. Seattle

Dear D. Seattle,

We all procrastinate from time to time. I, for example, received your email in the spring of 2007. Forgive me if in the interim you have solved your dilemma, but it is possible that my answer will still be useful.

I think we can postulate a utility function along the following lines: having a Christmas tree up during the Christmas season brings positive utility, but diminishing marginal utility over time. After a while, the marginal utility is negative: the tree becomes an irritation, offering neither use nor ornament.

Given that parsimony is a virtue in economic modelling, let us assume that if the tree (presumably plastic) survives the year, its presence at the following Christmas will not seem like old news, but will be as welcome as ever. Assume also that putting up the tree and taking it down bring disutility, although in my experience this is not necessarily the case.

All these simplifying assumptions create a bias towards leaving the tree up; despite that, working through a few numerical examples suggests to me that in almost all cases you are better off taking the tree down. Even now, in early December, I would advise you to dismantle your festive foliage and enjoy the thrill of renewing it on Christmas Eve.

If the tree is still up, I would suggest that your problem is deeper than poor cost-benefit analysis: it is a profound tendency to put off action that is troublesome in the short term. We have developed an institution to deal with this. It is called the New Year's resolution.

Yours festively,
The Undercover Economist

Dear Undercover Economist,

At the apartment block where I used to I live, I once parked in another tenant's car bay for a brief period. The tenant called the wheel clampers and landed me with a $120 (£69) fine, despite the fact he doesn't have a car and there were thirty spare car bays, and despite knowing that the car belonged to me. Up to that point I had had no run-ins with this person.

The tenant gained nothing from this except my bad opinion, and I was $120 worse off. Why did he not either ignore my car, or come up and knock on my door and say: 'Look, I've got these people on the phone who will clamp your wheels unless you persuade me otherwise.' He could have had a few bottles of beer out of it. But he didn't. So what was the rational reason behind his action?

– Jeremy Cook

Dear Jeremy,

You are right to be puzzled. Clearly, this neighbour did not maximise the value of his bargaining position in the narrow situation you describe. Still, I think there is a certain logic to what happened.

Game theory is the economist's tool of choice to analyse what happens when two or more people have to negotiate, cooperate, compete or otherwise engage with each other. The essence of game theory is that each side would expect the other side to anticipate and respond to his likely actions.

Game theory shows that there are times when irrationality (real or feigned) is a highly effective strategy. Someone who seems impervious to logic is someone who also gets his own way a lot. Consider, for example, toddlers, terrorists, bosses, dogs and the late Charles de Gaulle.

Your neighbour may have calculated that by demonstrating a willingness to punish you for no immediate personal gain, he will gain in the long term anyway. Irrational perhaps, but rationally irrational.

Yours vindictively,
The Undercover Economist

Dear Undercover Economist,

In the women's individual gymnastic competition at the Olympics, there were a couple of controversies over scoring that experts believe cost the US gymnast a gold. The problem is that officials from the top countries cannot be judges if a citizen from their country is in the competition, so the remaining judges are from countries with no gymnastic tradition. Is there an efficient way to solve this problem?

— Doney Joseph, Los Angeles, CA

Dear Doney,

In a sport whose entire aim is to win the approval of the judges, error is unavoidable. Yet (as the sports economist Stefan Szymanski reminds me) there is a trade-off here between two sorts of error: bias and variance. The decision to use disinterested but inexperienced judges should reduce bias but increase the variance of the outcome. That is a painful trade-off.

National pride is not the only source of bias. Judges have friends; they may know athletes, or their coaches. It was for this reason that the great US orchestras began to introduce 'blind auditions', where musicians performed behind a screen. The idea was to eliminate favouritism towards the students of particular teachers. The unexpected result – shown by the economists Claudia Goldin and Cecilia Rouse – was to disarm sexism as well as favouritism: many more women succeeded in the blind tests.

Alas, gymnasts can hardly perform behind a screen, although I suppose they could compete in balaclavas. All I can recommend is an alternative reward system for judges. Each should assign scores in isolation, and then be paid only if the other judges

297

agreed. The judges will need to coordinate on a 'focal point' if they wish to be paid, and the obvious focal point is their honest opinion of a gymnast's performance.

This is surely worth a try. If the judges cannot agree, of course, they will be paid exactly what they deserve: nothing.

Yours competitively,
The Undercover Economist

AFTERWORD

When the first edition of *Dear Undercover Economist* was published, I was wracked by doubt. Of course, as an economist I have always been more of a facts and figures man than a feelings and human frailties type. But even I worry about my effectiveness.

And so I wrote to some of my correspondents to ask them what they made of my advice, whether they took it and how things worked out. Many of them jumped at the opportunity to have their say, and their responses were first published in the *Financial Times* in August 2009. For the sake of straight-dealing and transparency, their rather mixed reactions are also contained in the pages that follow.

Dear Undercover Economist,

I believe that there is an inexplicable shortage of sex. Given that studies show that women and men enjoy it more than most other activities, and given its intrinsically low cost, it appears that even a crude approximation of a utility-maximising person would probably spend much more time having sex than most. Do you know of any economic discussion of this?

– Michael Vassar, New York

Dear Michael,

It is true that there is something puzzling about the lack of sex in the world. Everybody says they enjoy sex, you can do it fairly safely for the price of a condom, and all you need is somebody of the appropriate gender and sexual preference. How difficult can it be?

Economics professor and blogger Tyler Cowen has offered an embarrassment of possible explanations. In the spirit of perfect competition between economic pundits I suggest that you need fewer answers.

We need just two complementary theories, one to explain the all-night-long sex that couples aren't having as much of as they should; and the other to explain the casual sex that strangers should be having with each other, and aren't.

For couples, it's surely a case of diminishing returns. Just because the average utility of sex is high, doesn't mean that the marginal utility of more sex is also high. I enjoy sex but I am no longer a teenager and, to be blunt, it takes me days to reload. For strangers, the risk of rejection, violence or social condemnation seems very high. In groups where these risks are lower (gay men, students, hippies) my theory predicts that more sex should be going on.

There is a simpler explanation, though: everybody is having constant, guilt-free sex. They just haven't told the economists.

Michael Vassar responds:

Your response was far more fun than asking a sex columnist why people don't have enough money would be, but possibly grabs the low-hanging fruit while leaving a substantial proportion of the effect unexplained. That's the disciplinary standard though. Economists are prone to looking at the direction of an effect and mostly ignoring its magnitude, rather than proposing experiments to measure that magnitude. I'm happy with just the existence of such a column anyway.

December 17, 2005

Dear Undercover Economist,

I recently noted that I only really fancy my girlfriend after I've had a few drinks. Is this relationship worth pursuing?

– David Pigeon, London

Dear David,

I know how you feel: I only fancy chips with mayonnaise. Sadly for my waistline, my relationship with chips has not suffered. You are saying that like chips and mayonnaise, alcohol and your girlfriend are complementary goods. I am not sure this is a problem.

It might be a problem if your predicament were unusual. It is not. Many people have found that alcohol has aphrodisiac qualities.

Of course, it is easy to drink more alcohol than is good for you, but there should be no need for worry. The government advises that the average man should drink no more than three to four 'units' of alcohol. Since the typical British couple claims to make love every three days or so, you should be able to lubricate yourself appropriately without putting too much strain on your liver.

It seems to me that there is one cause for concern: your girlfriend must never suspect that you need to don the beer goggles to find her appealing. Drinking is commonplace in our culture, so you shouldn't find it hard to camouflage the limits of your infatuation. Just don't do anything stupid, such as discussing it in the pages of a national newspaper.

David Pigeon replies:

I followed your advice in the knowledge that I had one of the finest economic brains in the country at my side to steer me through the relationship. However, you omitted to advise that the beneficial effect of alcohol in enhancing sexual charms diminishes over time. I soon found that I required ever greater quantities in order to maintain interest and this took considerable toll on both my health and my pocket. I also encountered situations where no alcohol was available but had little explanation for my refusal of my partner's advances.

Nevertheless, all was for the best. We split up, but I'm now with a wonderful partner who I think I love, but who irritates and annoys me when she gets drunk. Any advice?

———

June 17, 2006

Dear Undercover Economist,

Why do most of us iron our clothes, when we are untidy in so many other ways?

– Judith Oliver, Singapore

Dear Judith,

There is an obvious difference between an immaculate shirt and an immaculate sitting room: you get to enjoy the aesthetic benefits of tidying your living space, but not – unless you spend a lot of time in front of the mirror – the aesthetic benefits of your own clothes.

After all, how many of you can honestly say you haven't sailed through the day, only to discover that you have spinach between your teeth and you forgot to brush your hair? The horror is apparent to everyone but you.

So why do we care more about other people's enjoyment of our tidiness than our own? It is not a matter of selflessness: we try to make a good visual impression because it will bring us wealth, status and, we hope, a bit of sex, too.

But a second question arises: why are we judged on appearances? It might be intrinsically satisfying to have a well-dressed boyfriend, but there is nothing fundamentally less productive about a scruffy accountant. Evidently, the tie is important because employers believe it is correlated with diligence and talent.

If this is true, we would expect to see the largest premium on snappy dressing in professions where there are few other effective ways to evaluate performance. Estate agents and management consultants are sharply dressed in the absence of more convincing guides to their competence.

In professions where talent is more obvious, this facade is not needed. That is why when I scan the *Financial Times* office, neatly pressed shirts and blouses are hard to find.

Judith Oliver replies:

I've been trying to picture Robin Lane Fox, my favourite FT columnist, in an un-ironed shirt, whether in a garden or in an Oxford tutorial. And it has been difficult. I thought of writing to ask him but I'm afraid he might think it a dreadful impertinence. Luckily, I have no doubt about his vast knowledge and talents.

August 11, 2007

Dear Undercover Economist,

I have just joined a dating website in the hope of finding true love. Friends of mine have started dating someone they met online, only for a 'better offer' to arise on the website. If this happens, what should I do?

– Duncan, London

Dear Duncan,

Internet dating allows more offers to be considered, so the tried-and-tested rules of thumb may no longer be appropriate. It might seem natural simply to consider how many offers you must sample until you are likely to meet 'Ms Right'. That would be naive. You must instead balance the benefits of choice against the effect your flightiness may have on your targets.

These decisions are much like those faced by a company choosing the optimal number of suppliers. Dealing with more suppliers allows the company to choose the cheapest and best. But having too many makes suppliers insecure and unwilling to invest in the relationship.

Your ideal choice depends on what you want. Fun and frolics are ideally obtained by keeping options open, perhaps even switching to the spot market. But if you want your partner to have your babies, support you while you write your novel or share the cost of buying a home, you will need to reassure her that you do not have other competitors waiting in the wings.

In some industries it is common to sign contracts with two suppliers – enough competition to keep each on its toes, but enough commitment to inspire big investment in the relationship. In your case that would be a wife and a long-term mistress. Perhaps the tried-and-tested rules of thumb work after all.

Duncan replies:

I was very grateful for your advice. I am delighted to report that I am now happily married, and so is my mistress.

Dear Undercover Economist,

I am in doubt whether it is worth changing school
for my last year of A-levels. I would be living in a
much better place (Cambridge, whereas I am now in
Dover) and getting more tuition. I am likely to have
better accommodation, more freedom and will meet
people with diverse interests. But is it worth the
risk of not getting into university or getting lower
grades on my A-levels? Please help me to solve this
dilemma.

– G.P., Dover

Dear G.P.,

Let us run through this supposed dilemma again. You are considering a move to a place that appears to be better in every
dimension, including the academic one. Yet you are hesitant
because of a perceived risk.

I am tempted to suggest you consult a shrink rather than an
economist. Fortunately, so-called behavioural economists combine the best qualities of economist and psychologist. And any
behavioural economist would quickly diagnose that you are a
victim of the 'endowment effect'.

The endowment effect is an irrational preference to keep what
you have – better the devil you know and all that.

A typical experiment designed to reveal the effect would give
participants a small gift for participating in the experiment.
Later, the participants would be invited to swap the gift for an
alternative. No matter what the original gift was, or what the

alternative is, people, irrationally, are reluctant to make the swap.

Your attachment to substandard lodgings and scant tuition in Dover is clearly irrational. Move to Cambridge at once. You may be wrong, of course, but a risk of error is no excuse for inaction.

G.P. responds:

I am very thankful for your advice as it has helped me to achieve one of my academic goals. I have followed it: I left my old college in Dover last January and went to a sixth-form college in Cambridge. This was all to get into the University of Cambridge, which had rejected me. I was lacking the courage to go for a change, but your logical explanation of the situation was decisive.

At the end of it all, not only did I make lots of new friends and do well in my exams, but I managed to get into Cambridge – to read economics – on my second attempt! I am now preparing for my first year.

Again, thank you very much for your influence.

———

June 14, 2008

Dear Undercover Economist,

I am about to be married, and have no doubts about the relationship. But there is one nagging worry: my fiancé co-owns a condo overlooking the Pacific Ocean near San Francisco – with an ex-girlfriend, who lives next door to it. She is not in a position to buy him out of his

investment, and although they rent it out, the mortgage
is steep. I believe the condo is an investment specific to
the former relationship and would like it divested – but
the housing market is a shambles.

– Mary, USA

Dear Mary,

While I sympathise with your problem, I must correct you. A
relationship-specific investment is one that is worth more within
a relationship than outside it, such as a set of wedding photos.
The condo is not relationship-specific, just unprofitable and
illiquid. The condo can therefore be disposed of without destroying value – but not, it seems, by either side buying the other side
out.

If your fiancé sold his share to a stranger, he'd sell at a
loss. But, in truth, the loss has already happened; his reluctance
to sell suggests he's pig-headed as well as an incompetent
investor.

So I recommend that you buy out your fiancé's share, at a fire-
sale price. Subsequent negotiations about the condo would then
be between you and the ex. Should your marriage work out, you
can share the profits with your fiancé. And if not, at least you will
have prearranged some compensation.

*Mary admitted that she had not taken my advice, and invited her
fiancé (still not married?) to respond.*

He writes:

*My stake in the flat is essentially a free-call option. My renters'
payments cover the mortgage payments, and the asset has already*

lost its value. Upside awaits. What I didn't take into account were the externalities: an indignant fiancée, a difficult ex and an illiquid market. My biggest regret is not securitising those risks, representing them as assets and selling them to the major US banks.

Acknowledgements

I am flattered at the number of readers who assume 'Dear Economist' was my idea. It wasn't. The column began in the *FT Magazine* a few weeks before I penned my first words for the *Financial Times*. Therefore I am particularly grateful to Martin Wolf and Chrystia Freeland, who hatched the idea together, to Alan Beattie and Chris Giles, who wrote the first few brilliant columns and set the tone for things to come, and to Pilita Clark, my first 'Dear Economist' editor, who invited me on board. Since then Graham Watts, Mike Skapinker, Isabel Berwick, Andy Davis and Sue Norris have all done sterling work in editing the column and keeping it fresh. I'm also very grateful to Lionel Barber and Dan Bogler for making it possible to publish this book.

I'm grateful to Lindsey Schwoeri, Ryan Doherty and Iain Hunt for important help in organising the book, and as always to my agent Sally Holloway, to my editors Tim Bartlett and Tim Whiting, and to Andrew Wright for skilfully ironing out my rumpled introductions.

Above all I want to thank the readers who send in such fantastic and inventive questions every week. Some of you are strange people, and that's a great thing.

Finally thank you to my beautiful, clever and very patient wife, Fran Monks. It is not easy being married to an economist who cites Gary Becker and Avinash Dixit during domestic arguments. May we continue to make the right decisions together.

Now you can order superb titles directly from Abacus

☐ The Undercover Economist   Tim Harford   £8.99
☐ The Logic of Life   Tim Harford   £8.99

The prices shown above are correct at time of going to press. However, the publishers reserve the right to increase prices on covers from those previously advertised, without further notice.

───────────── ⬭ABACUS⬭ ─────────────

Please allow for postage and packing: **Free UK delivery.**
Europe: add 25% of retail price; Rest of World: 45% of retail price.

To order any of the above or any other Abacus titles, please call our credit card orderline or fill in this coupon and send/fax it to:

Abacus, PO Box 121, Kettering, Northants NN14 4ZQ
Fax: 01832 733076   Tel: 01832 737526
Email: aspenhouse@FSBDial.co.uk

☐ I enclose a UK bank cheque made payable to Abacus for £ . . . .
☐ Please charge £ . . . . . . to my Visa/Delta/Maestro

Expiry Date ☐☐☐☐   Maestro Issue No. ☐☐

NAME (BLOCK LETTERS please) . . . .

ADDRESS . . . .

. . . .

. . . .

Postcode . . . . Telephone . . . .

Signature . . . .

Please allow 28 days for delivery within the UK. Offer subject to price and availability.